THE COOKBOOK

Volume 1

masterChef
NEW ZEALAND

THE COOKBOOK

Volume 1

RANDOM HOUSE
NEW ZEALAND

A RANDOM HOUSE BOOK published by
Random House New Zealand
18 Poland Road, Glenfield, Auckland,
New Zealand

For more information about our titles go to
www.randomhouse.co.nz

A catalogue record for this book is available
from the National Library of New Zealand

Random House New Zealand is part of the
Random House Group
New York   London   Sydney   Auckland
Delhi   Johannesburg

First published 2010

© 2010 MasterChef is a trade mark of
FremantleMedia Australia Pty Ltd as agent for
Reveille LLC dba ShineReveille

ISBN 978 1 86979 369 2

countdown
shop smarter

Photoshoot food supplied by Countdown

Incidental photography: Frances Oliver
Food photography: Aaron McLean
Food styling: Marc Zajtman and Ginny Grant
Design: Anna Seabrook

Printed in China by Everbest Printing Co Ltd

Contents

Foreword

When most of us filled out the application form for *MasterChef New Zealand* the last thing we were thinking about was television cameras. Neither did we give a thought to what life would be like during the challenges nor how we would cope under the most extreme pressure (I certainly didn't forget garlic and ginger on purpose!). We did, however, want the chance to learn from some of the country's finest chefs. The top sixty all got to taste the pressure, the top twenty-four began to dream of things to come and finally the top twelve made it to the house.

We all loved food; there was always something to talk about and something to share. We could do nothing other than talk and eat, eat and talk. Our love of food enabled twelve strangers to settle in together and become friends amid a fierce competition.

I embraced — and grew from — the experience with its challenges and eliminations. So it is little wonder that I now feel that I've been through something special, something that changed me, and I am sure the others feel this too.

This competition at times seemed harsh. It was most definitely real. The three wise men stood strong and, at times, they seemed threatening. Their knowledge was impressive and palates even sharper — we all knew that we had to perform every time. In this competition you were only as good as your last dish.

MasterChef New Zealand was full of tears, sweat and passion and it was a show for the whole family. The *MasterChef* phenomenon got kids thinking about cooking and families back into the kitchen.

This book aims to inspire those of you at home who have a burning desire to cook, the desire to transform your food world one dish at a time. This book is full of fantastic creations just waiting to be cooked. Enjoy!

Brett McGregor,
New Zealand's first MasterChef

Stock your pantry

What do you cook for dinner when all you've got in the house is a pork chop, half a block of dark chocolate, some flat-leaf parsley, a quarter of a cabbage and a bread roll? While being able to improvise a fabulous meal from whatever ingredients are on hand is an enviable skill and the true test of a resourceful cook, keeping the pantry stocked with basic staples makes the job a lot easier.

Dry ingredients

A pantry should be cool, well ventilated and not exposed to direct bright light. Once packages are opened, the contents should be transferred to airtight containers. Make sure you label them to avoid any confusion, and try to keep track of how long you have had them. The keeping times given below are a general guide – check the use-by dates on the packet. Don't buy large quantities unless you are using them regularly. Also, try to rotate ingredients by using up the contents of containers before topping up from a new packet.

Flour: keep for up to 9 months
Standard flour: for pastry, biscuits, sauces, gravy, dusting meat, chicken and fish.

High grade flour (bread flour): for bread, pizza bases and pasta.
Self-raising flour: for cakes, puddings and other baking.
Cornflour: for sauces, sponges and some desserts.

Cocoa powder: keep for up to 1 year
Look for dark cocoa (also known as Dutch cocoa), which gives a deep, rich colour to chocolate desserts and baking, and looks great dusted over a finished dessert.

Sugar and sweeteners: keep indefinitely
Caster sugar: good for use in baking and desserts, as the smaller grains dissolve quickly.
Brown sugar: gives a slightly more caramel flavour and a darker colour to the finished product.
Demerara sugar: has large, golden-brown granules, and gives a slightly different colour, flavour and texture.
Golden syrup: has an intense sweetness and mild treacly flavour that works well in baking and desserts.
Honey: can add subtle, complex flavours, rather than just the bland sweetness of sugar. Try to keep it uncontaminated by using only clean utensils to spoon it out. If honey crystallises, sit the jar in hot water.
Icing sugar: good in icings, and where a fine texture is desired, as in some pastry. Also used as a garnish, dusted over a finished dessert or baked product.

Coconut: keep for up to 12 months
Available desiccated, shredded or flaked. Desiccated coconut is most commonly used in baking. If using coconut as a garnish or topping, lightly toast it in a dry frying pan for a golden colour and nutty flavour.

Rolled oats: keep for up to 12 months
Use in baking and desserts, as well as porridge and muesli.

Breadcrumbs: keep for up to 6 months
Dried breadcrumbs can be used to crumb meat, fish and chicken. For real crunch, try Japanese breadcrumbs, called panko, which are a coarse crumb, similar in size to fresh breadcrumbs, but dry and crisp.

Dried fruit: keep for up to 12 months (check individual packages for dates)
Sultanas, raisins, apricots, cranberries, figs, dates . . . there are many types of dried fruit and they often appear in savoury as well as sweet dishes, as they marry particularly well with rich meat and game.

Nuts and seeds: keeping times vary; check use-by dates
Nuts have a wide variety of uses – from baking to sauces, or just sprinkling over a finished dish. Because of their fat content they are quite perishable and should be purchased in small quantities. Keep in a cool, dark place, or in the fridge if you won't use them up within a couple of months.

Dried pulses: keep for up to 12 months
Dried lentils, beans, chickpeas and split peas are useful pantry additions, though they usually need to be soaked overnight before cooking.

Pasta and noodles: keep for up to 2 years
Dried pasta forms the base of a quick meal at any time. Keep a variety of shapes in the cupboard – spaghetti, penne, linguine – and some lasagne sheets, too. Dried noodles, rice vermicelli and mung bean vermicelli are great for Asian dishes, as are rice-paper wrappers and nori sheets for sushi rolls.

Rice: keep for up to 12 months (brown rice for 9 months)
Basmati: for pilaf, or to accompany Indian curries.
Jasmine: to accompany Asian-style dishes.
Medium grain: for desserts or paella.
Arborio, carnaroli or vialone nano: for risotto.
Sushi or short-grain rice: for sushi.
Brown rice: for salads, or as an accompaniment.

Couscous: keep for up to 2 years
Instant couscous is a handy pantry staple which can be used to accompany a curry or flavoursome stew, or as the basis of a more substantial side dish or salad.

Polenta: keep for up to 12 months
Polenta is a good, filling staple. You can make it and let it set in the fridge, then cut it into pieces and fry or grill it until crisp. Alternatively, a soft polenta can be served like mashed potatoes with a casserole or stew.

Dried herbs and spices: whole spices up to 2 years; ground spices and dried herbs up to 9 months
Herbs and spices should be bought in small quantities, as they soon lose their fresh aroma and flavour. For the best result, buy whole spices and grind them yourself. Keep salt and black pepper on hand for grinding and use white pepper for sauces.

Canned goods

Cans should have no dents, rust or damage, as the seal may be affected and the contents unsafe. Most cans have use-by dates, but as a general rule they should be used within 12 months of purchase. Unused portions of canned goods should be transferred to another container, covered and refrigerated for up to 2 days.

Some canned products are fine, and others should be avoided at all costs! The following are useful, tasty and make good stand-by pantry ingredients.

Tomatoes: check use-by date
Canned tomatoes are great for cooking when fresh tomatoes are out of season. Italian-style diced tomatoes make a quick, easy addition to casseroles, soups and stews, and an excellent base for pasta sauce.

Tuna and salmon: check use-by date
Canned fish is handy for fish cakes, sandwiches, pasta, salads and pies.

Beans, chickpeas and brown lentils: check use-by date
The quickest way to use pulses is from a can, as they don't need soaking. Just drain into a sieve and rinse under cold running water. Use them in soups, curries, stews, salads and side dishes.

Coconut milk and coconut cream: check use-by date
Canned coconut milk and cream are vital ingredients in many South-East Asian dishes.

Fruit: check use-by date
A lot of fruits aren't available year round, especially short-season varieties such as apricots. Canned fruits are best used in puddings and pies.

Bottles and jars

Sauces in glass bottles will keep longer than those in plastic. Some products, such as oils, are sold in green or brown glass bottles as the contents will spoil if exposed to the light. These should be kept in a dark corner of the pantry. Most bottles and jars should be refrigerated after opening (check the label if you're not sure), and keep an eye on the use-by date.

Oil: keep for up to 12 months, depending on the type
Flavourless vegetable oils (such as sunflower or canola): for deep-frying, or cooking at high temperatures.

Olive oil: imparts a subtle flavour and is good for some simple pan-frying, though it has a low 'smoke point', which means it can burn at high temperatures.

Extra-virgin olive oil: prized for its flavour and colour, and often used in dressings or drizzled over a finished dish. It keeps longer when stored out of direct light.

Peanut oil: commonly used in stir-fries for its flavour and high smoke point.

Sesame oil: added as an 'extra' to impart its distinctive flavour to other oils and in salad dressings and sauces.

Fridge and freezer

Vinegar: keep for up to 2 years (though a harmless sediment may form in the bottom of the bottle)

Vinegar is used for salad dressings, or to deglaze a pan after frying meat, chicken or fish. A good-quality red wine vinegar, a white wine vinegar and balsamic vinegar are always useful in the kitchen. Herbed vinegars are good for salad dressings, while rice vinegar and Chinese black vinegar are called for in many Asian dishes.

Mustard: keeping times vary (check use-by date and refrigerate after opening)

A Dijon and wholegrain mustard will cover most cooking needs. Use mustard in salad dressing, or add to the pan after deglazing to make a simple sauce. Hot English mustard serves as a delicious condiment with meat.

Asian sauces: keeping times vary (check use-by dates and refrigeration requirements)

Different Asian cuisines call for their own particular sauces and condiments. The many varieties of soy sauce and fish sauce are invaluable for marinades, soups and stir-fries, along with condiments such as kecap manis, hoisin and teriyaki. Keep prepared wasabi in the fridge for sushi and sashimi.

Cheese: keep soft cheese up to 5 days, cheddar up to 3 weeks, Parmesan up to 6 weeks

Cheeses for cooking (as opposed to the gorgeous artisan cheeses you buy for the sheer pleasure of eating them) are easy to keep on hand and have many uses. A good cheddar, Parmesan, feta or creamy blue can elevate a dish such as a simple omelette to a whole new level. When you've removed a cheese from its packaging, wrap it in waxed paper and keep it in the crisper section of the fridge.

Butter, cream, sour cream: check use-by dates

Dairy products are perishable but will keep in the fridge for a reasonable amount of time. Butter can be frozen.

Eggs: keep up to 5 weeks, though use as soon as possible

When purchasing eggs, look for the carton with the longest use-by date. The date stamped on the carton is 6 weeks after the eggs were first packed. Store in the fridge in the carton. Choose free-range eggs for the best flavour and colour, and if you can find a source of fresh eggs, all the better!

Pastry: keep for up to 3 months after opening

Nothing matches pastry made from scratch, but at a pinch frozen pastry can come in handy. Shortcrust and puff pastry are available in sheets so you can take what you need and keep the rest frozen. Make sure it is tightly wrapped to prevent freezer burn.

Vegetables: keep up to 6 months in the freezer

Not many purchased frozen vegetables are great, but peas and spinach are two that are acceptable and useful to have on hand. Make sure opened packages are tightly sealed.

Ice-cream: keep for up to 3 months

A tub of good-quality vanilla ice-cream in the freezer means that dessert is never an issue! Drizzle with some melted dark chocolate, or top with fresh seasonal fruits, chopped nuts or toasted coconut. Serve with a homemade fruit pie or just on its own.

Flavour heroes

Keep any or all of these on hand to liven up the simplest meal.

Capers: keep for up to 6 months in the fridge after opening
Pickled or salted, baby or large, capers provide a burst of intense flavour. Rinse salted capers before use.

Olives: keep for up to 2 weeks in the fridge after opening
Green, stuffed, Kalamata, Ligurian, Sicilian . . . for best flavour, buy olives that haven't been pitted.

Anchovy fillets in oil: keep for up to one week in the fridge after opening
Drain and chop or mash to dissolve into a sauce or stew.

Semi-dried or sundried tomatoes: keep opened jar in the fridge and use within 2 weeks
Keep a jar of sundried tomatoes ready in the cupboard to toss through pasta or onto a pizza.

Fresh ginger: keep in the fridge for up to a week
Sliced, chopped or grated ginger adds another layer of flavour to a stir-fry or marinade.

Chillies
Chillies can be used fresh or dried as chilli flakes or chilli powder.

Lemons and limes: keep limes up to a week and lemons up to a fortnight, or refrigerate for a longer life
The juice and finely grated zest of lemons or limes can be used in many dishes, sweet and savoury. To have lemon juice ready at hand, freeze the fresh juice in ice cube trays, then store in a snaplock bag in the freezer.

Herbs: grow them fresh and pick the leaves as you need them
The best way to have fresh herbs on hand is to grow them yourself. Even the teensiest balcony can accommodate a pot or two of your favourite herbs.

Vanilla: pods keep for up to 6 months; vanilla extract keeps indefinitely
The divine flavour and fragrance of vanilla will lift any baking or dessert. Use a good vanilla extract when making cakes or baked products. Vanilla pods are great when used where the distinctive tiny seeds can be seen – in sauces, custard or ice-cream.

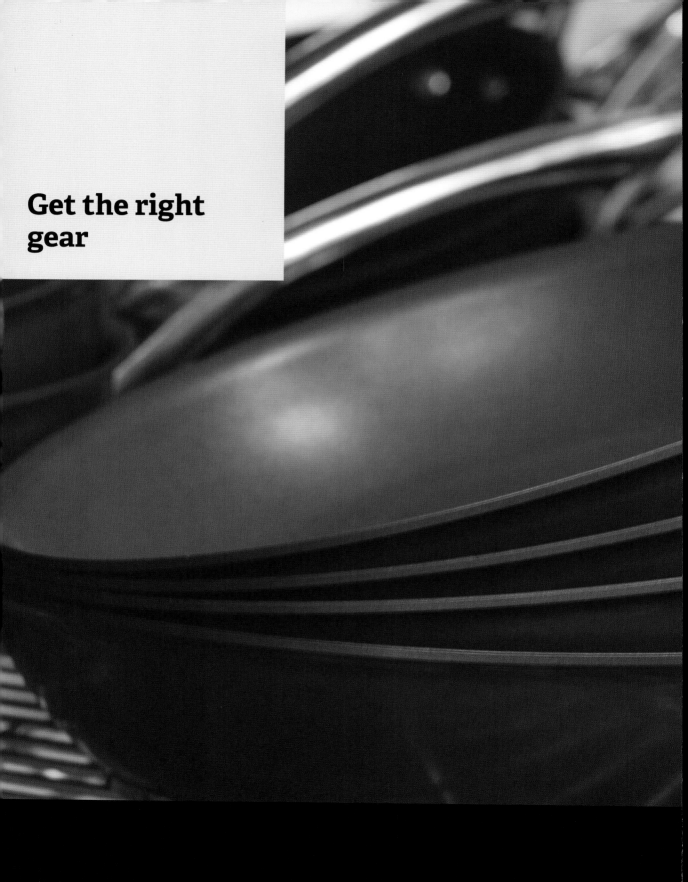

Get the right gear

It's easy to go mad in kitchenware shops, surrounded by all those gleaming pots and pans, chunky mortars and pestles, sharp knives, and shiny high-tech gadgets. What do you really need, though?

Equipment basics

Knives

Fancy knife sets in attractive blocks are widely available, but you could spend a fortune and end up only using one or two of them. Better to invest in a couple of good-quality knives and build from there. Look for knives with blades that extend to the end of the handle, embedded or riveted into the handle material. A knife should have a good weight and 'feel' in your hand.

You will need a large chef's knife, wide at the base, with a blade about 20 centimetres long. These knives are versatile, suited to a whole range of jobs, from chopping carrots to carving a chicken.

A paring knife is useful for small jobs, such as peeling and trimming vegetables.

A serrated bread knife is best for cutting bread without squashing it. You will also need a steel to keep your knives sharp. Do this by running each side of the blade at a slight angle down the steel.

Occasionally you will need to have your knives professionally sharpened. You will know it's time to do so when the effects of using the steel don't last long. Ask at a kitchenware shop – they should be able to recommend someone.

Boards

Chopping boards come in a variety of materials, such as wood, plastic, marble or glass. Marble and glass aren't particularly good for your knives and are more decorative than functional.

Many commercial kitchens use plastic chopping boards these days, often colour coded to prevent cross-contamination. This means using one colour board for meat, another for vegetables, and so on. If you don't want to keep a rainbow of chopping boards on hand, simply remember that cooked food should never be placed on a board that has recently been used to cut raw meat, chicken or fish.

Plastic boards and wooden boards with a coarse grain often end up scored with deep cuts that can harbour bacteria. Ideally, choose wooden boards with a tight grain (preferably end grain) and always be scrupulous about scrubbing boards in hot soapy water after use. Rinse well, wipe dry and stand in a well-ventilated place to dry completely.

Pots and pans

A few good-quality saucepans in varying sizes are an excellent start when you're kitting out your kitchen. The number of pans you need will depend on the number of people you regularly cook for. Go for at least a couple of medium-sized saucepans, a small saucepan and a large stockpot for cooking pasta, soups and stews.

A heavy base is essential, as it distributes heat evenly and prevents scorch spots. Stainless steel pans with a copper base were once the pan of choice, but today there are many new materials and non-stick surfaces available. Look for reputable brands and feel for weight.

A steamer add-on is often available with saucepans. This perforated pan sits over a saucepan of water and cooks vegetables by steaming, a method which preserves colour, shape and nutrients.

Ovenproof frying pans (with metal rather than plastic handles) are convenient, as food such as meat can be seared in the pan, then placed in the oven, still in the pan, to finish cooking. Just don't forget that the handle will be hot after being in the oven.

A chargrill pan is a heavy, ridged pan which sits over the flame and replicates a barbecue grill. High-end cooktops often have these built in. They contribute a slight smokiness to food, and the grill lines give an attractive look for presentation.

Flameproof casserole dishes transfer easily from cooktop to oven, which makes them convenient, as you can do all the initial browning on the stove and then place it in the oven for long, slow cooking. A good one will be quite heavy and made from enamelled cast iron, which distributes and retains heat extremely well.

If you don't have a flameproof casserole dish, you can brown your meat, onions and any other ingredients in a frying pan, then transfer them to a casserole dish for baking.

Woks

A wok is necessary if you do a lot of Asian cooking. It can be used for stir-frying, simmering, deep-frying and steaming. There are many different types of woks available now, made from a range of materials. Some have a non-stick surface, and you can even get electric woks, which are handy if you have a small stovetop. Round-bottomed woks work well on gas stoves, though you may like to use a ring under the wok to keep it stable. Flat-bottomed woks are best for electric stoves.

What you choose will depend on your preferences and budget, but a basic steel wok, available from Asian specialty shops and kitchenware shops, is good. These woks are coated to keep them from rusting before being sold, so they need to be prepared and seasoned before use. Scrub with a scouring pad and hot soapy water to remove the protective film. Heat the wok and wipe the interior surface all over with peanut oil (use paper towels, and be careful). Repeat with more oil and paper towels until the wok leaves no residue on the paper.

Once seasoned, never wash your wok with detergent. Just use hot water and a brush to clean. Dry thoroughly before storing.

Measuring

Even the most confident cook will need to measure ingredients at some point – particularly for baking, where precision is important.

Use a glass or plastic jug with levels clearly marked on the side for measuring liquids.

Scales are the most accurate way to measure dry ingredients. Digital kitchen scales give the most accurate weight, usually to the gram. Sometimes a recipe will give only cup measurements, in which case a simple set of cup measures, in ¼, ⅓, ½ and 1 cup sizes, comes in handy.

Measuring spoons come in sets of ¼, ½, 1 teaspoon and 1 tablespoon. In New Zealand (and the UK) a tablespoon is 15ml. Be aware that in Australia a tablespoon is 20ml.

Other tools

Wire rack: used to cool cakes and biscuits so they don't become soggy on the base.

Rubber spatula: made from flexible rubber or heatproof silicone on a wooden handle, these versatile tools are used for folding, scraping, stirring and lifting.

Wooden spoons: used for stirring, and particularly good on non-stick surfaces. You'll need a couple of different sizes and shapes. Some cooks like to keep one spoon for sweet and another for savoury.

Metal spoons: wide metal spoons are good for skimming. Slotted spoons have holes so you can lift food from water or oil, and wide Chinese-style metal spoons are great for folding and scooping.

Ladles: deep, long-handled spoons for serving soups and stews.

Tongs: handy for turning, or for lifting food from hot oil or water.

Balloon whisk: a bulbous wire whisk used to aerate food, such as egg whites, or to beat sauces to create an emulsion.

Egg slice: a wide, thin, rigid metal or silicone blade on a long handle for turning foods such as eggs, pancakes or fish in a frying pan.

Masher: used to mash potatoes and other vegetables.

Pastry brush: for brushing uncooked pastry with glaze, such as milk or beaten egg. Also good for brushing oil or melted butter onto filo pastry.

Piping bags: used to pipe meringue or choux pastry and to decorate cakes and biscuits. Nozzles of various sizes and shapes help keep your portions uniform and your presentation neat.

Cutters: metal cutters in varying shapes and sizes are handy when cutting pastry shapes or making biscuits or scones. These can rust, so make sure you dry them thoroughly before storing after use.

Machinery

Food processor: invaluable for chopping and shredding, making pastry, pasta and pesto, or for puréeing vegetables, soups and sauces.

Blender: can be used to purée, though it tends to aerate mixtures. Great for drinks.

Stick blender: purées soups and sauces in the pan, which saves transferring mixtures from a pan to a food processor and back.

Electric beaters: these can be hand-held beaters, or a free-standing machine. Used for creaming butter and sugar, for whipping cream, beating egg whites and many other foods.

Spice grinder: can be used in place of a mortar and pestle to grind small amounts of spices or to make pastes.

Bowls

Stainless steel or glass are best, as plastic tends to be hard to clean properly. Egg whites are very difficult to beat to a good volume in a plastic bowl.

Grating

A box grater with coarse and fine holes is useful. Microplanes come in various degrees of coarseness, and are excellent for grating zest, nutmeg, chocolate and Parmesan cheese.

Cake tins, trays and baking dishes

Cake tins: to start, invest in a couple of basic round tins. Standard sizes are 20cm and 23cm (the diameter is measured across the base). Cake tins with non-stick finishes are common now, but it is still advisable to grease or line them to prevent sticking.

Springform tins: these cake tins have a spring clasp on the side, allowing you to expand the side and lift it from the base without disturbing the top of the cake. This is good for cakes with decorative toppings baked on, and for cheesecakes and deep pies or tarts.

Small cake tins: muffin, patty cake and friand tins are readily available. If you're not using paper cases, line the bases with small pieces of non-stick baking paper.

Loose-bottomed flan tins: great for pastry-based tarts or quiches. These flan tins consist of a ring (usually fluted) and a flat base that fits inside it. After cooking, the ring can be slipped off the base for appealing presentation and ease of portioning. To remove the base, carefully slide a large palette knife between the pastry and the metal base to loosen. Gently slide the tart onto a serving plate.

Trays: flat baking trays can be used to bake everything from scones and biscuits to vegetables, nuts, meat, fish and chicken. Because they have no sides, the heat circulates evenly around the food.

Soufflé dishes: round ceramic dishes with straight sides to help the soufflé rise during cooking. These are available large, or small for individual serves.

Ramekins: usually ceramic, glass or pottery dishes, in single-serve sizes for baked or chilled desserts or savoury dishes.

Baking and casserole dishes: large, deep dishes with a lid to seal in moisture, usually ceramic or made from glass or pottery, and used for cooking casseroles or stews in the oven.

Shallow baking dishes: useful for baked pasta or vegetable dishes such as potato bakes. They can be rectangular, round or oval and are usually about 6cm deep. They have a large surface area for creating a delicious brown crust on food.

Roasting pans: usually made of metal, and large enough to accommodate a big piece of meat such as a whole chicken or a leg of lamb, sometimes with vegetables around it (though roast vegetables can be cooked in a separate dish). Being metal, they can be placed over a flame to make gravy from the pan juices while the meat is resting. Roasting pans are also used to cook food in a bain marie; the roasting pan is filled with water, smaller dishes are placed in it, and the whole thing is placed in the oven to cook.

Strainers

Colander: made from enamel, stainless steel or plastic, these are great for draining pasta, rice or vegetables.

Sieve: wire mesh sieves are used for draining solids from liquid.

Small sieve: useful for dusting dessert dishes with icing sugar or cocoa powder for presentation.

Chop, slice and dice

As judge Ross Burden says, 'Remember, in the kitchen, your knives are your best friends.' The basis of all good cooking begins with a knife and a board. So, how are your knife skills?

Basic knife skills

Using a knife is all about balance. Stand with both feet flat on the ground, square to your chopping board. Grip the handle firmly. Rest the blade against the back of the fingers of your other hand, keeping your fingertips tucked safely away.

Start with a slow, even rhythm. As you practise you will build up speed. After a while, you will become very attached to 'your' knife, so much so that any other knife will feel strange in your hand. A knife is a chef's main tool and becomes almost a part of them.

Slicing
Always keep your fingertips curled back, away from the blade of the knife.

Chopping
When chopping herbs, use a rocking motion and keep the tip of the knife on the board.

How to dice an onion

1 To dice an onion, cut it in half lengthwise, then turn it so the root points to your left and slice towards, but not through, the root. (If you are left-handed, point the onion's root to the right instead.)

2 Slicing parallel to your chopping board, cut towards, but not through, the root once more, taking care at all times to keep your fingers away from the blade. Start at the base and work up, repeating 2–3 times.

3 Finally, slice vertically again from right to left.

How to julienne a carrot

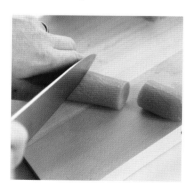  

1 To julienne a carrot, first cut it into even lengths, about 3cm long.

2 Next cut it lengthwise into 2mm-thick slices.

3 Finally, cut each slice lengthwise into 2mm-thick strips.

How to dice a potato

1 To dice a potato, slice off the rounded edges to square it up.

2 Cut into even 1cm–2cm slices.

3 Cut each slice into even 1cm–2cm batons.

4 Cut each baton into 1cm–2cm cubes.

Make your food look good

Whether you're hosting a cocktail party at the Langham Hotel, throwing together a meal for the food critics from *Cuisine*, or just making some toast to eat in front of the TV while you watch a cooking show, presentation is crucial. 'We eat with our eyes,' was a common refrain from the *MasterChef* judges. So how do you make food look delicious?

We eat with our eyes

The love and passion you put into preparing and cooking a dish should follow through when you are plating it up – whether you are cooking for one, serving the weekday family meal or having a dinner party. We taste with our eyes first, so let the dish shine.

Some restaurant food is like going to the opera – it's a show, it's about wowing the audience, it's imaginative, creative and inspirational. The food is plated like a work of art, with a smear of sauce, a slice of this and a dollop of that. Restaurants use those large, elegant white plates for a reason. They're like a blank canvas. There's no reason why you can't achieve the same look at home – but some of your family, friends or guests might privately wonder, 'Where is the rest of my dinner?' The key is finding a balance between the generosity of a homemade meal, cooked with love, and the wow factor of a restaurant dish.

There are no hard-and-fast rules when plating food. It's personal, and everyone has different taste. But professional chefs and food stylists have a few tips and tricks they use to take everyday dishes to the next level, simple ideas you can use when plating up your own culinary creations. Make your food a visual masterpiece, as well as a culinary triumph.

Style food with height

Body, shape and ooze can make an ordinary dish look mouth-watering. For example, meat and three veg may look more appealing if the four ingredients are stacked in a juicy tower on the plate and drizzled with sauce.

If you have a chunky soup, spoon the ingredients in a mound in the centre of the bowl. Pour liquid in around them so they jump out visually, rising like an island from the sea.

Garnishes can work miracles

Take a cookbook down off the shelf and look at the pictures. Nearly every main course dish will be garnished with a sprig of parsley, roughly torn basil leaves, chopped coriander or artfully arranged chives. It's because green lifts a dish visually, adding freshness and colour. Finely sliced chillies and spring onions cut on the diagonal are often used for the same reason.

Sauces and oils are also favourites with food stylists for their visual appeal – they make food glisten.

Garnishes do more than make a dish look more exciting, though. They add extra depth, making the flavours come together and completing the meal.

Make the diner feel special

Individual small portions and little extras make the person you are feeding feel special.

Complete the meal at the table

Just serving a dish with an accompanying sauce in a jug and then pouring it over at the table gives a meal a personal touch. Flambéing a pudding or dessert has the same effect. Though they may not recognise it, your guests will feel they have been part of something, that you have somehow included them in the making of the dish.

Let the food speak for itself

Sometimes a dish just is what it is, and the best garnish is no garnish at all. Think of the tradition of Mediterranean food, in which the hero ingredient is often presented on its own. You may be served a piece of meat on a plate, perhaps with a wedge of lemon. It's the beauty of the food that makes a dish like this appealing. No need for stacking or smearing!

Cook the basics

Vegetable stock

Makes 2½ litres
Preparation time: 15 minutes
Cooking time: 1 hour

1 onion, chopped
2 leeks (white part only), chopped
4 carrots, chopped
4 sticks celery, chopped
1 bouquet garni
10 black peppercorns
12 cups (3 litres) water

1 Bring all the ingredients to a simmer (not boil) in a stockpot, then adjust the heat and simmer, uncovered, for 1 hour.

2 Cool slightly. Strain.

3 Refrigerate or freeze in portion sizes.

Note If you like, roast the vegetables until slightly caramelised before making the stock. This will give it a deeper flavour.

Chicken stock

Makes 2½ litres
Preparation time: 15 minutes
Cooking time: 2 hours

2kg chicken carcass and bones
  (cooked or raw)
2 onions, chopped
2 carrots, chopped
3 sticks celery, chopped
1 bouquet garni
10 black peppercorns
14 cups (3½ litres) water

1 Bring all the ingredients to a simmer (not boil) in a stockpot, then adjust the heat and simmer, uncovered, for 2 hours. Skim any froth from the surface occasionally as it cooks.

2 Cool slightly. Strain.

3 Refrigerate the stock, uncovered, overnight. Skim off the fat, then refrigerate or freeze in portion sizes.

Note Cooked chicken carcass and bones will give a slightly deeper flavour than raw chicken. It makes good use of the remains of a roast chicken.

Beef stock

Makes about 2 litres
Preparation time: 15 minutes
Cooking time: 3½ hours

2kg beef bones
2 carrots, chopped
2 onions, chopped
3 sticks celery, chopped
2 tomatoes, chopped
1 bouquet garni
10 black peppercorns
14 cups (3½ litres) water

1 Preheat the oven to 200°C (180°C fan-bake). Spread the bones onto an oven tray and roast for about 30 minutes until well browned.

2 Bring the beef bones and remaining ingredients to a simmer (not boil) in a stockpot, then adjust the heat and simmer, uncovered, for 3 hours. Skim any froth from the surface occasionally as it cooks.

3 Cool slightly. Strain.

4 Refrigerate the stock, uncovered, overnight. Skim off the fat, then refrigerate or freeze in portion sizes.

Seafood stock

Makes about 1¾ litres
Preparation time: 15 minutes
Cooking time: 30 minutes

2kg fish bones, heads and tails
2 sticks celery, chopped
1 onion, chopped
1 leek, chopped
1 carrot, chopped
1 bouquet garni
10 black peppercorns
8 cups (2½ litres) water

1 Bring all the ingredients to a simmer (not boil) in a stockpot, then adjust the heat and simmer, uncovered, for 30 minutes.

2 Cool slightly. Strain.

3 Refrigerate or freeze in portion sizes.

Note Prawn and lobster heads, tails and shells may be added to the stock, as well as crab shells.

Vinaigrette

Makes ⅓ cup (80ml)
Preparation time: 5 minutes
Cooking time: nil

1 tbs white wine vinegar
1 tsp Dijon mustard
3 tbs olive oil
salt and freshly ground black
   pepper

1 Whisk the vinegar and mustard together in a small bowl.

2 Gradually whisk in the oil.

3 Season with salt and pepper.

Note This basic vinaigrette can be varied in many ways. White wine vinegar can be substituted with red wine, balsamic, raspberry or herb-infused vinegars. For a light, fruity vinaigrette, replace the vinegar with lemon, lime or orange juice.

Shortcrust pastry

Makes 1 base (double the quantity
  for base and lid) for a 24/25cm tin

1⅓ cups (200g) plain flour
125g chilled unsalted butter, diced
1 egg
1 tbsp water
½ tsp sea salt

1 Process the flour and butter in
a food processor until the mixture
resembles fine breadcrumbs. Add
the egg, water and sea salt and
process until the mixture comes
together to form a smooth ball.
Press the pastry into a disc, wrap in
clingfilm and chill for 15 minutes or
longer if you have time.

2 When the pastry is required, roll
out and line a tin. Trim the edges
and chill again for 30 minutes.

3 Preheat the oven to 165°C.

4 Prick the pastry with a fork and
line with baking paper. Fill with
rice or baking beans to 'blind bake'.
Bake for 15–20 minutes until lightly
golden. Then remove the rice and
continue to bake for 5–8 minutes.

Sweet shortcrust pastry

Makes 1 base (double the quantity
  for base and lid) for a 24/25cm tin

1½ cups (225g) plain flour
¼ cup (45g) icing sugar
pinch of salt
125g chilled unsalted butter, diced
2 egg yolks

1 Process the flour, icing sugar,
salt and butter in a food processor
until the mixture resembles
breadcrumbs. Add the egg yolks
and process until the pastry just
forms a smooth ball. Press into
a flat disc and wrap in clingfilm.
Refrigerate for 15 minutes or longer
if you have time.

2 When the pastry is required, roll
out and line the tin. Trim edges and
chill again for 30 minutes.

3 Preheat the oven to 165°C.

4 Prick the pastry with a fork and
line with baking paper. Cover with
rice or baking beans to 'blind bake'.
Bake for 15–20 minutes until lightly
golden. Then remove the rice and
bake again for 5–8 minutes.

Pasta dough

Makes 12 tortellini or 6 ravioli

200g plain flour of tipo '00' fine
  Italian flour
pinch of salt
2 eggs, lightly beaten
olive oil

1 Place the flour and salt in a food
processor and pulse to combine.
With the motor running, add the
eggs and process until combined.
Drizzle in a little olive oil and
continue to process until a springy
dough forms. Remove from the
processor and place on a clean,
lightly floured surface and knead
for 5 minutes or until smooth and
elastic. Wrap in clingfilm and set
aside to rest for 30 minutes.

2 Lightly flour a pasta machine.
Divide the pasta dough into
quarters and keep pieces covered
until ready to use. Roughly flatten
out one quarter, about the width
of the pasta machine, dust with
flour, then pass through a pasta
machine, starting with the thickest
setting. Adjust the roller setting
down a notch, and pass the dough
through 2 or 3 times. Repeat with
the remaining dough, working fast
so the pasta doesn't dry out, lightly
dusting the dough with the flour if
it sticks until finishing on the finest
setting. Lay the sheets out flat and
cut into the required shape.

How to . . .

How to choose the right potato

There are so many types of potato available that sometimes it is hard to know which one is best for the job.

Floury potatoes are high in starch and low in moisture. They are best for mashing, baking, roasting and for chips. The most common examples are Agria, Ilam Hardy and Red Rascal.

Waxy potatoes are higher in moisture than floury ones and hold their shape when boiled without going mushy. They are great for salads. The most common examples are Nadine, Draga and Frisia.

All-purpose potatoes sit in the middle of waxy and floury, and are suitable for most cooking methods. The most common examples are Rua, Desiree and Karaka.

New potatoes are fresh, young potatoes. They aren't necessarily small, but usually have a thin, papery skin. A great example is Jersey Bennes.

How to skin a tomato

1 Score a cross into the skin on the base of the tomato.

2 Place in a heatproof bowl and cover with boiling water. Stand for a couple of minutes until the skin begins to lift. Remove from the water.

3 Cool slightly, then peel away the skin.

4 Cut the top off the tomato and scoop out the seeds with a teaspoon.

How to joint a chicken

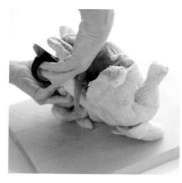

1 Take a very sharp knife or a pair of scissors and cut through the parson's nose.

2 Stand the chicken on its end and insert the scissors into the cut you've just made, then cut straight down the chicken's back.

3 Open the chicken out flat, skin side down, and cut through the breastbone.

4 Turn each half over, stretch out the legs and cut them away from the breast.

5 If you need 6 portions, take the breast portion and cut it in half, removing the wing.

6 If you need 8 portions, take the legs and cut through the thin white line running down the middle of the joint.

How to carve a chicken

1 Using a sharp knife, cut between the leg and the body to remove the thigh and drumstick together.

2 Remove the wing on the same side.

3 Slice the breast meat.

4 If you need 2 leg portions, cut through the joint between the thigh and the drumstick.

How to fillet a fish

1 Take a whole fish that has been gutted and scaled. Pat dry with absorbent paper so it isn't too slippery. Using a sharp knife, make a cut on a 45-degree angle, just behind the gills and under the fin, where the head meets the body. Score through the flesh on both sides, then cut right through the bone to remove the head.

2 Cut along the backbone, feeling where the flesh joins the bone, easing to lift the meat from the ribs. Cut at the tail end to release the flesh from the tail.

3 At the top of the spine, cut through the small bones that attach the flesh.

4 Lift off the fillet. Repeat with the other side.

5 Lay the fillets skin side down and cut a sliver from the top of the fillet to remove the tiny belly bones. Run your knife over the skin to make sure no scales remain.

6 To remove the pin bones, feel where the small ribs are and pull out with tweezers. Support the flesh with your fingertips so you don't tear it.

How to extract crayfish meat

1 Twist the head and tail of the cooked crayfish in opposite directions.

2 Remove the tail fins and gently break the shell, trying not to break off or tear any of the flesh.

3 Extract the tail meat in one piece.

4 Separate the top from the bottom of the body, remove the legs and break open the joints where the legs meet the body.

5 Pick the meat out of the joints, then break open the legs and extract the meat.

6 Using a mallet, break open the antennae to get the meat from them.

Nibbles

Pan-fried scallops, cauliflower purée, and pear and sultana chutney

Langham Hotel
Serves 4
Preparation time: 15 minutes
Cooking time: 40 minutes

Cauliflower purée

500g cauliflower, chopped
400ml milk
125g butter, diced
salt to taste
30ml cream

Pear and sultana chutney

2kg pears, peeled, cored and diced
120g glucose
120g caster sugar
½ tsp cinnamon
200g sultanas
1 vanilla pod

oil for frying
40 scallops
micro-greens for garnish

1 To make the cauliflower purée, place the cauliflower in a saucepan, add the milk and put over a medium heat. Bring to the boil and cook until tender.

2 Once cooked, drain the cauliflower, reserving the milk. Place the cauliflower and butter in a food processor and process until smooth. Season with salt to taste. Add a little of the reserved milk and the cream and process until smooth. Allow to cool.

3 To make the pear chutney, place the pears, glucose, sugar, cinnamon, sultanas and vanilla pod in a saucepan over a medium heat and simmer until pears are tender.

4 Heat an oiled frying pan over a high heat and sear the scallops for 20–30 seconds on each side (or longer, depending on size), turning them only once.

5 To serve, spoon the purée into small bowls. Top with a scallop, followed by the chutney and garnish with micro-greens.

The beautiful Atlantic scallops we cooked on the show are a lot harder to cook than our own New Zealand scallops, as they are much larger, so they need pan-searing with a little olive oil, butter, sea salt and pepper and to be finished off in the oven quickly. They are ready when they are only just warm inside — any less and they aren't cooked enough, any more and they turn into rubber bullets. You really need that caramelisation on the scallops to get that beautiful flavour happening.

A tip: use a smoking hot pan, and only drop in a little butter once you've turned the scallops onto the second side, otherwise the butter just burns.

The reaction to these scallops when they were delivered to the party-goers was amazing — they really loved them! And the scallops worked beautifully with the pear and sultana chutney and the cauliflower puree — yum! What's not to love? **Steve Juergens, Langham Challenge**

Goat's cheese ravioli with date and fig chutney, and sage butter

Langham Hotel
Makes 20
Preparation time: 30 minutes to
  chill pasta dough plus 20 minutes
Cooking time: 30 minutes

Pasta dough
300g Italian tipo '00' flour
pinch of salt
2 egg yolks
2 eggs
1 tbsp olive oil

Date and fig chutney
175ml apple cider
175ml white wine vinegar
125g brown sugar
100g dates, cut into 4mm dice
1 Granny Smith apple, peeled, cored
  and cut into 4mm dice
3 cloves garlic, finely chopped
2 tsp grated ginger
450g figs, cut into 4mm dice
½ tsp ground cardamom
½ tsp salt

Goat's cheese filling
250g goat's cheese, crumbled
30g walnuts, toasted and chopped
30g basil leaves, chopped
1 tbsp extra-virgin olive oil
2 tsp minced garlic
1 tsp grated lemon zest
1 tbsp honey

Sage butter
100g butter
20 sage leaves

1 To make the pasta dough, place the flour and salt in a food processor. Add the egg yolks and eggs, and process until combined. With the motor running, drizzle in a little olive oil and continue to process until a moist dough forms. Remove from the processor and place on a clean, lightly floured surface and knead for around 5 minutes until smooth and elastic. Wrap in clingfilm and set aside to rest for 30 minutes.

2 To make the chutney, place the cider, vinegar and brown sugar in a saucepan and put over a high heat. Bring to the boil, stirring until the sugar has dissolved. Reduce the heat to medium, then add the dates, apple, garlic and ginger and cook for 15 minutes or until most of the liquid has been absorbed. Stir in the figs, cardamom and salt. Set aside.

3 To make the filling, combine all the ingredients in a bowl and set aside.

4 To make the ravioli, take one-quarter of the pasta dough and roughly flatten it out. Dust with flour, then pass it through a pasta machine, starting with the thickest setting and finishing with the finest. Repeat with the remaining dough, working fast so the pasta doesn't dry out. Lay the sheets out flat and cut out discs of 7–8cm diameter using a pastry cutter.

5 Place a teaspoon of the filling in the centre of a disc and wet the edge of the round with water. Place another disc on top and press the edges together, removing any air. Repeat with the remaining pasta and filling.

6 Place a frying pan over a medium heat and cook the butter for 3–4 minutes until just starting to turn brown. Add the sage leaves and cook for 1 minute or until crisp. Remove the sage leaves and drain on a paper towel. Reduce the heat and continue to cook the butter until golden brown.

7 Bring a saucepan of salted water to the boil, add the ravioli in batches and cook for 4–5 minutes or until the ravioli float to the surface. Remove with a slotted spoon and drain.

8 Serve the ravioli drizzled with sage butter, topped with the chutney and garnish with a fried sage leaf.

This recipe always gets rave reviews! The lemon, garlic and basil will ensure the flavour of the dish still comes through while the slight crunch of the walnuts contrasts perfectly with the soft cheese and pasta. **Kirsty Cardy, Langham Challenge**

Beer-battered fish and chips

Langham Hotel
Serves 4
Preparation time: 30 minutes to
chill batter plus 10 minutes
Cooking time: 15 minutes

Batter
225g self-raising flour
1 egg, lightly whisked
375ml light beer or larger, chilled
salt and freshly ground black
pepper
vegetable oil for deep-frying

6 Russet potatoes (if not avaibable
use Agria), peeled and cut into
finger-sized batons
4 x 120g white fish fillets
lemon wedges for serving

1 To make the batter, place the flour in a bowl and add the egg, stirring to combine. Pour the beer in gradually, whisking to make a smooth batter. Season with salt and pepper. Cover the bowl with clingfilm and place in the refrigerator for 30 minutes to rest.

2 Half fill a large saucepan with oil and heat to 180°C. Deep-fry the chips in batches for 5–6 minutes until light golden. Remove with a slotted spoon and drain on paper towels. Cool to room temperature.

3 Cut each fillet of fish into 2 pieces. Coat 2 pieces of fish in batter, drain off the excess, then deep-fry for 3–4 minutes until golden brown. Drain on paper towels. Repeat with the remaining fish and batter.

4 Finish the chips by deep-frying for 2–3 minutes or until crisp. Drain on paper towels.

5 Fill 4 paper cones with 2 pieces of fish each and some chips. Season with salt and tuck in lemon wedges.

The trick to great beer-battered fish 'n' chips is to use a good quality beer and most importantly make sure it is ice cold! Fresh fish is a must and make sure you don't over-cook it. The judges commented that I did not use enough salt. So it is very important to salt the fish and chips. Ross's top tip was to place the chips in a stainless bowl and toss them with salt! **Rob Trathen, Langham Challenge**

Lamb skewers with capsicum relish

Langham Hotel
Makes 20–25 skewers
Preparation time: 30 minutes
Cooking time: 40 minutes

500g minced lamb
1 egg
30g breadcrumbs
100g raisins
80g pine nuts, roasted and chopped
30g fresh chillies, de-seeded and
    finely chopped
salt and freshly ground black
    pepper
wooden or bamboo skewers, soaked

Capsicum relish
1 tsp orange oil
200g red capsicums, cored and
    finely diced
200g yellow capsicums, cored and
    finely diced
100g mango, peeled, seeded and
    finely diced
1 tsp mustard seeds
100ml chicken stock
1 tsp Thai red curry paste
1 tbsp sweet chilli sauce
½ tsp sweet smoked paprika

1 To make the lamb skewers, combine the minced lamb with the egg, breadcrumbs, raisins, pine nuts and chilli in a bowl. Season with salt and pepper and mix well. Shape into 8cm-long rolls and insert a skewer through the middle of each. Set aside.

2 To make the capsicum relish, heat the orange oil in a saucepan over a medium heat. Sauté the red and yellow capsicums and mango until soft. Stir in the remaining ingredients and cook for 15 minutes. Remove the pan from the heat and allow to cool.

3 Heat an oiled frying pan to high and sear the lamb skewers on all sides until lightly brown.

4 Preheat the oven to 180°C. Place the skewers in the oven for 8–10 minutes to finish cooking, then remove and rest for 5 minutes.

5 To serve, arrange the lamb skewers on a platter with the relish in a bowl alongside.

I really loved the capsicum relish that went with these skewers. It was delicious and I think it was the real star of this dish.
Brett McGregor, Langham Challenge

Entrées

Mozzarella, prosciutto and tomato with Saporosa balsamic

Ellerslie Race Day
Serves 2
Preparation time: 15 minutes

4 slices prosciutto di Parma
2 balls fresh buffalo mozzarella,
  sliced into 4
2 vine-ripened tomatoes, sliced
  into 4
small handful fresh basil leaves
extra-virgin olive oil
Saporosa or other good-quality
  balsamic vinegar
sea salt and freshly ground black
  pepper

1 Place the prosciutto diagonally on a plate and top alternately with the mozzarella and tomato slices. Scatter the basil leaves over, and drizzle with olive oil and balsamic vinegar. Season with salt and pepper.

Although this recipe didn't require cooking, it was still difficult. The key was getting the right balance of flavours and presentation. Everything had to be beautiful and uniform and that was never my strong point on the show. My favourite thing about this dish was getting to use Simon's personal 150-year-old fully-restored hand meat-slicer. It was really an honour to work with such a great piece of machinery. But it was also tough work turning the crank over and over again to get the delicate slices of prosciutto that were required. Great care was needed when cleaning it — the blade was razor sharp.
Karyn Fisk, Ellerslie Challenge

Seared yellowfin tuna with fennel salad and salmon caviar

Ellerslie Race Day

Serves 4

Preparation time: 10 minutes

Cooking time: 1 hour

2 small to medium sized bulbs
 fennel

juice of 1 lemon

2 preserved lemon quarters, flesh
 discarded and peel cut into 3mm
 dice

1 x 350g–400g yellowfin tuna loin

olive oil for frying

salt and freshly ground black
 pepper

lemon oil for drizzling

small handful micro-cress

salmon caviar for serving

1 Using a mandolin, shave the fennel bulbs into thin slices. Place in a bowl of cold water with a squeeze of lemon juice. Put the preserved lemon in another bowl. Place both in the fridge.

2 Heat an oiled frying pan over a high heat until very hot. Brush the tuna with olive oil and season with salt and pepper. Sear the tuna loin for 1–2 minutes on each side, turning it as you go. It should have a crust, but remain raw in the centre. Remove the tuna from the pan and cool in the freezer for 45 minutes.

3 When the tuna is cool enough to handle, cut it into 5mm-thick slices. Lightly wrap in clingfilm and form into a cylindrical shape, and twist the ends.

4 Drain the fennel and combine with the preserved lemon. Drizzle with lemon oil and carefully mix together.

5 To serve, arrange the tuna slices in the centre of a plate, overlapping the edges. Top with a small handful of fennel salad and some micro-cress. Scatter with salmon caviar, and drizzle with lemon oil.

What an absolutely beautiful dish. Fantastic fresh tuna loin seared, then wrapped in clingfilm to keep its shape. Served with some Swiss red chard and watercress with a beautiful preserved lemon dressing, it was a beautiful dish to look at but even better to eat. It was just a shame that I left a little piece of clingfilm on it and a customer found it. This is something I would cook again. Everyone who tried it loved it.
Steve Juergens, Ellerslie Challenge

Snapper and mussel chowder

I have prepared seafood chowder for my family and friends for many years. My good friend and fishing buddy Gary Evans refused to waste anything from a fishing trip, so he taught me to perfect a great fish stock using the frames from the snapper we filleted. This chowder is fantastic; it is one of those dishes that succeeds through its simplicity, with a minimum of herbs, spices and flavours.

Recipe by Nigel Anderson
Serves 4
Preparation time: 30 minutes
Cooking time: 45 minutes

30 green-lipped mussels in the
   shell, cleaned and de-bearded
2 cups white wine (Chardonnay)
1 whole snapper
4 tbsp olive oil
1 onion, chopped
2 sticks celery, diced
2 carrots, peeled and diced
8 black peppercorns, crushed
5 sprigs parsley
1 golden kumara, peeled and finely
   diced
75g butter
75g plain flour
100ml cream
salt and freshly ground black
   pepper
4 sprigs dill
8 slices ciabatta

1 To steam the mussels, place the mussels in a large saucepan, pour in the wine and cover. Place the pan over a medium-high heat and allow the mussels to steam open, discarding any that don't. Strain the liquid and set aside. Remove the mussels from the shells and place in a bowl to cool. Finely chop half the steamed mussels, removing the beards. Chop the remaining mussels into 3–4 pieces and set aside.

2 To prepare the fish, fillet, skin and de-bone the snapper, reserving the head and bones, but discarding the eyeballs, gills and scales. Slice each fillet into 4 pieces.

3 To make the stock, place the olive oil in a large saucepan over a medium heat. Sauté the onion, celery and carrot until soft, then add the snapper head and bones and just cover with water. Add the peppercorns and parsley, and simmer for 15 minutes.

4 Strain the liquid through a fine sieve into a large clean saucepan, pour in the reserved mussel liquid and place over a medium heat. Add the kumara and simmer for 10 minutes or until tender. Remove the kumara and set aside.

5 Melt the butter in a small saucepan over a low heat. Add the flour, allow to bubble, then stir continuously for 3–4 minutes, being careful not to burn the mixture.

6 Add the fish stock, 2 ladles at a time, to the butter and flour mixture, whisking continuously until the sauce is lump free and coats the back of a spoon. Place the chopped kumara into the stock and cook for 10 minutes.

7 Just before serving, add the fish fillets, mussels and cream and poach gently for 2–3 minutes until the snapper is just cooked. Taste and season with salt and pepper.

8 Ladle the chowder into heated soup bowls, give each a grind of pepper and top with dill sprigs. Serve with warm ciabatta.

Italian grilled mussels with tomato sauce

Recipe by Kelly, Nigel & Tracey
Serves 4
Preparation time: 35 minutes
Cooking time: 50 minutes

20 green-lipped mussels in the
  shell, cleaned and de-bearded
½ cup white wine
30g butter
2 cloves garlic, crushed
1 x 400g tin crushed tomatoes
1 tbsp white sugar
1 tbsp Saporosa or other good-
  quality balsamic vinegar
1 tsp dried Italian herbs
1 bay leaf
fresh basil leaves, torn
salt and freshly ground black
  pepper
1 cup breadcrumbs
grated zest of 1 lemon
2 cloves garlic, crushed
½ cup grated Parmesan
lemon wedges for serving

1 To steam the mussels, place the mussels in a saucepan, pour in the wine and cover. Place over a medium heat. Bring to the boil, then reduce to a simmer, allowing the mussels to steam open, discarding any that don't. Strain the liquid and set aside. Remove the mussels from the shells, place in a bowl, and clean the shells.

2 To make the sauce, heat a frying pan over a medium heat, add the butter and sauté the garlic until soft. Add the tomatoes, reserved mussel liquid, sugar, balsamic vinegar, Italian herbs and bay leaf, and simmer for 20–25 minutes. Add the basil leaves and cook for a further 1–2 minutes. Season with salt and pepper.

3 Preheat the oven grill to hot. Combine the breadcrumbs, lemon zest, garlic and Parmesan in a bowl.

4 Arrange the mussel shells on a baking tray and place a cooked mussel in each shell. Spoon the tomato sauce over and top with the breadcrumb mixture. Grill until golden.

5 Serve the mussels on a platter with lemon wedges.

This is a dish I cook regularly for my family. We are mindful of how good seafood is for us and mussels can be obtained fresh anywhere in the country at any time. I believe mussels are under-utilised and, at the same time, spectacular value. The dish I cooked in the challenge featured a standard Italian-style tomato sauce inside the shell, with the cooked and cleaned mussel on top. This was then topped with a mixture of dried breadcrumbs, melted butter, grated Parmesan cheese, lemon zest and salt and pepper, then grilled until heated through and golden. We did have a minor issue on the day because we didn't know we were cooking on a barbecue. Therefore, we didn't quite get the colour on the crumb topping that we would have liked, but it was still a pleasing result — both the mussels and the challenge.
Nigel Anderson, Villa Maria Challenge

Koura broth with a taste of Asia

Recipe by Kylie Wheeler
Serves 4
Preparation time: 10 minutes
Cooking time: 50 minutes

2 x 450g–500g crayfish
2 tbsp chopped ginger
4 shallots, finely chopped
2 cloves garlic, finely chopped
4 stalks lemongrass, bruised and
  finely sliced
3 long red chillies, de-seeded and
  finely sliced (reserve half for
  garnish)
6 kaffir lime leaves, finely sliced
  (reserve some for garnish)
2 tbsp peanut oil
6 cups fish stock
2 tsp grated palm sugar
2 tbsp fish sauce
½ cup Riesling
juice of 2 limes
2 spring onions, julienned
50g coriander leaves, chopped

1 Place the crayfish in a large pot of well-salted boiling water and cook for 8 minutes. Remove and put in ice-cold water for 4–5 minutes. When cool, remove the head by twisting the head and tail in opposite directions. Using scissors, cut down each side of the tail on the underside of the shell to remove the meat, carefully keeping it whole (see page 53). Cut the meat into 1cm slices. Clean the guts from the head and retain the body shells, head and legs.

2 To make the stock, heat a frying pan over a low heat and sauté the ginger, shallots, garlic, lemongrass, chilli and lime leaves in the peanut oil for 5 minutes. Add all the crayfish shells, head and legs, and sauté for a further 5 minutes. Add the fish stock and palm sugar, and simmer for 20 minutes. Strain the stock into a clean saucepan.

3 Add fish sauce, Riesling and sliced crayfish meat to the stock and cook for a few minutes to heat through.

4 Ladle the soup into bowls and squeeze lime juice over. Top with spring onion, coriander and the reserved chilli and lime leaves.

This recipe was inspired by my travels in Asia. I now like to experiment in the kitchen and often attempt to create new dishes with exotic flavours I have discovered on my travels.

I live on the West Coast (Taranaki) where there is crayfish aplenty and my dad and his friends go diving for crays whenever the weather is right, so it's almost a staple in our diet! I tried out this particular dish for my friends, but used fish, and they loved it. For the competition, I decided that the crayfish would make it a little bit inspired. I don't use recipes often and when I cook I add a dash of this and a dash of that, so each time I make this dish it comes out differently. My presentation wasn't too flash on the day, which was disappointing, but I was pleased when Ray McVinnie commented that I had a very good understanding of Asian flavours.

Chinese crunchy chicken and pork (san chow bow)

Recipe by Mark Harvey
Serves 2
Preparation time: 20 minutes
Cooking time: 5 minutes

3 skinned and boned chicken thighs
100g pork mince
1 tbsp sesame oil
¼ tsp salt
⅛ tsp freshly ground black pepper
2 tbsp finely chopped spring onions
2 tbsp finely chopped water
  chestnuts
1 tbsp finely chopped garlic
2 tbsp oil
¼ cup white wine
2 tsp oyster sauce
2 tsp soy sauce
½ cup bean sprouts
1 cup crisp noodles
iceberg lettuce leaves for serving

1 Mince the chicken thighs in a food processor. Combine the chicken and pork with the sesame oil, and salt and pepper. Leave to marinate while you prepare the spring onions, water chestnuts and garlic.

2 Heat a wok to high and add the oil. Fry the chicken and pork until brown. Then add the spring onions, water chestnuts, garlic, white wine, oyster and soy sauces, and stir-fry for a further 2–3 minutes.

3 Add the bean sprouts and crisp noodles just before serving, reserving some for garnish. Toss together.

4 To serve, spoon the stir-fry mixture into the lettuce leaves, and top with bean sprouts and crisp noodles.

The name of this dish is something I had to come up with on the fly because of my pantry meltdown on the show where I forgot the lettuce. This should be served in a lettuce cup and sprinkled with bean sprouts and crisp noodles. I first tried this dish at a wonderful little restaurant called Monsoon Asian Kitchen in my home town, Palmerston North, many years ago and fell in love with it instantly. Despite my attempts to bribe the chef, Ken, for his recipe, he would not give it up. I've tried many variations of the dish since then and think this is the closest reproduction of his flavours I've managed to get.

Prawn and coriander dumplings

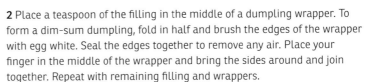

Recipe by Steve Juergens
Makes 12
Preparation time: 20 minutes
Cooking time: 10 minutes

12 medium raw prawns, shelled and
  de-veined
¼ cup chopped coriander leaves
  and roots
¼ tsp salt
¼ tsp white pepper
½ egg white, beaten
12 round dumpling wrappers
soy sauce for dipping

1 To make the filling, place the prawns, coriander, salt, pepper and half the egg white in a food processor. Pulse until just combined.

2 Place a teaspoon of the filling in the middle of a dumpling wrapper. To form a dim-sum dumpling, fold in half and brush the edges of the wrapper with egg white. Seal the edges together to remove any air. Place your finger in the middle of the wrapper and bring the sides around and join together. Repeat with remaining filling and wrappers.

3 Bring a saucepan of water to the boil and top with a tight-fitting bamboo steamer. Place the dumplings in the steamer and steam for 7–10 minutes or until the wrappers are translucent.

4 Serve immediately with soy sauce on the side for dipping.

I love yum cha! The myriad dishes that are served up in small bamboo steaming baskets really excite me — I love going to yum cha for dim sum! One of my faves is prawn and coriander dumplings, which is why I created this dish. The sweet, tender prawns marry perfectly with the beautiful aromatic coriander to create a taste explosion — yum! All you need is a little soy sauce for dipping and you're done. I had never made dumplings before, but we had a very enjoyable masterclass session with the chefs at China restaurant, who taught us the intricate art of folding pastry into dim sum — it is amazing to watch how fast they can do it, and they make up to 1000 dim sum a day!

Prawn gow gees with lemon dipping sauce

Recipe by Mark Harvey
Makes 12
Preparation time: 10 minutes
Cooking time: 10 minutes

canola oil for deep-frying
12 medium raw prawns, shelled and
   de-veined
1½ tsp finely chopped ginger
1½ tsp finely chopped garlic
3 tsp finely chopped spring onions
2 tsp soy sauce
dash of sesame oil
salt and freshly ground black
   pepper
round dumpling wrappers

Lemon dipping sauce
2 tsp sugar
½ cup lemon juice
4 tsp soy sauce
4 tsp brown sugar
½ cup chicken stock

1 Heat the oil in a deep fryer
to 180°C.

2 To make the gow gees, mince the prawns in a food processor, then mix
in a bowl with the ginger, garlic, spring onions, soy sauce, sesame oil, and
salt and pepper.

3 Place a heaped teaspoon of mixture in the middle of one dumpling
wrapper. To shape like a tortellini, fold in half, press the edges together,
removing any air, then place your finger in the middle of the wrapper and
bring the sides around and join together. Repeat with the remaining filling
and wrappers.

4 Deep-fry the gow gees for 5 minutes or until golden brown. Remove from
the oil with a slotted spoon and drain on paper towels.

5 To make the sauce, place all the ingredients in a saucepan over a
medium heat and bring to a gentle simmer. Reduce by one-third to a thick
and sticky consistency.

6 Serve the gow gees with the lemon sauce on the side.

*Simple flavours cooked well equals delicious! I use wonton wrappers
cut into circles and shaped like an Italian tortellini. The secret is
getting the oil temperature just right so the gow gees are crisp and not
drenched in oil. You might have to do a couple of test runs to get the oil
to the correct temperature but they should cook for about 4 minutes
and be a lovely golden colour when finished. Happy frying.*

Deep-fried boiled eggs with sweet and sour sauce

Recipe by Karyn Fisk
Serves 2
Preparation time: 15 minutes
Cooking time: 15 minutes

4 eggs
oil for frying
1 tsp finely chopped garlic
1 long red chilli, de-seeded and
  chopped into 3mm dice (reserve
  some for garnish)
¾ cup 3mm-diced carrot
½ tsp ground ginger
½ cup Shaoxing wine
2 tbsp light soy sauce
10g palm sugar
salt and freshly ground black
  pepper
canola oil, for deep-frying
spring onions, finely sliced on an
  angle, for serving

1 Place the eggs in a bowl and
cover with hot water for 3 minutes. (This sets the eggs.)

2 Place the eggs in a saucepan of salted boiling water and boil for
4 minutes. Remove and put in ice-cold water for 5 minutes. Peel when
cool.

3 Heat oil in a wok to high and stir-fry the garlic, chilli and carrot for
2 minutes.

4 Add the ginger, wine, soy sauce, sugar, and salt and pepper, and stir-fry
for a further 3–4 minutes until the liquid starts to thicken.

5 Heat the canola oil in a deep fryer to 180°C.

6 Deep-fry the peeled eggs for 3–5 minutes until golden. Remove with a
slotted spoon and drain. Slice in half.

7 Divide the sauce between 2 plates and place 4 egg halves on top of each
portion. Garnish with spring onion.

*This dish is great for those Sunday morning brunches when you're
worried that your cholesterol might be a bit on the low side. You can
have the sauce as hot or as mild as you want and it's great with some
crisp greens.*

Prawn wonton soup

Recipe by Karyn Fisk

Serves 4
Preparation time: 40 minutes
Cooking time: 30 minutes

Wontons

10 medium raw prawns, peeled,
 de-veined and roughly chopped
1 tsp Shaoxing wine
1 tsp soy sauce
1 tsp sesame oil
1 clove garlic, crushed
1 spring onion, finely diced
salt to taste
16 wonton wrappers

Soup

4 cups chicken stock
2cm piece ginger, peeled and sliced,
 plus 1 tbsp julienned for serving
2 cloves garlic, crushed
3 Chinese celery stalks, 2 chopped
 and 1 finely sliced
1 star anise
½ onion, finely diced
4 tbsp light soy sauce
¼ cup Shaoxing wine
1 spring onion, finely sliced
 lengthwise, plus 1 finely sliced on
 an angle for garnish

1 To make the wontons, combine the prawns, wine, soy sauce, sesame oil, garlic and spring onion in a bowl. Season with salt. Set aside to marinate for 30 minutes.

2 To make the soup, place the chicken stock, ginger, garlic, chopped celery, star anise and onion in a saucepan. Put over a medium heat and simmer for 15–20 minutes.

3 While the soup is simmering, assemble the wontons. Place wonton wrappers on a flat surface and place ½ teaspoon of filling into the centre of each wrapper. Fold in half, sealing the edges and removing any air. Place your finger in the middle of the wrapper and bring the sides around and join together.

4 Strain the stock into a clean saucepan, discarding vegetables and spice, add the soy sauce and wine and bring to the boil. Reduce to a simmer, place the wontons in the stock and simmer gently for 2 minutes or until the wontons are cooked. Add the spring onion, remaining Chinese celery and julienned ginger and cook for a further 1–2 minutes.

5 Ladle into bowls and garnish with spring onion.

Before MasterChef, if someone told me that I would one day make a prawn wonton soup, I would have laughed, yet this challenge landed me in the top two contestants of the day! I knew so little of Chinese cuisine before the show but now I love making Chinese food. The marriage of beautiful flavours and aromas like garlic, ginger, coriander, star anise, sesame oil and soy, complemented by crisp fresh vegetables and tender meat is a delight for all the senses. MasterChef definitely taught me not to be intimidated by foods that are different from what I'm used to. Plus, Chinese food is a great way of getting heaps of vegetables into your family. Lol!

Tasting plate: prawn spring rolls, pork and spring onion wontons, prawn dumplings and chicken feet

One of the highlights of the show for me was our trip to China — the Chinese restaurant in downtown Auckland where we spent a few hours with the chefs who taught us how to make dumplings, spring rolls and wontons. This challenge was a real turning point for me in the competition, as I decided against my usual urges to try something different and opted for the simple traditional methods, just as I had learnt at the restaurant. I won the challenge, which proves that simple and traditional food is sometimes the best.

Recipe by Kirsty Cardy

Makes 4 of each
Preparation time: 20 minutes
Cooking time: 2 hours, 15 minutes

Prawn spring rolls

canola oil for deep-frying
12 raw prawns, peeled, de-veined
and chopped
3 tsp finely chopped celery
1 tsp chicken stock
½ tsp sesame oil
salt and freshly ground black
pepper
4 spring-roll wrappers
egg white for sealing

Pork and spring onion wontons

canola oil for deep-frying
50g pork mince
1 tsp finely sliced spring onion
½ tsp sesame oil
½ tsp fish sauce
salt and freshly ground black
pepper
4 wonton wrappers
egg white for sealing

Prawn spring rolls

1 Heat the oil in a deep fryer to 180°C.

2 To make the filling, place half the prawn meat in a food processor and mince, or chop very finely. Place in a bowl with the rest of the prawn meat. Combine with the celery, stock, oil, and salt and pepper.

3 To assemble the spring rolls, place a wrapper on a flat surface and put a tablespoon of filling at one end of the wrapper. Roll, tucking in the edges to prevent oil penetrating the spring roll during cooking. Brush the end with egg white and seal. Repeat with the remaining filling and wrappers.

4 Deep-fry the rolls for 3 minutes or until golden. Remove with a slotted spoon and drain on paper towels.

Pork and spring onion wontons

1 Heat the oil in a deep fryer to 180°C.

2 To make the filling, combine the pork mince, spring onion, sesame oil, fish sauce, and salt and pepper in a bowl.

3 To make the wontons, place a teaspoon of filling in the bottom third of a wonton wrapper. Brush the edges of the wrapper with egg white and fold in half, sealing the edges and removing any air. Place your finger in the middle of the wrapper and bring the sides around and join together. Seal with egg white. Repeat with the remaining filling and wrappers.

4 Deep-fry the wontons for 4 minutes or until golden. Remove from the oil with a slotted spoon (or a spider – a wooden-handled mesh spoon) and drain on paper towels.

(continued overleaf)

Prawn dumplings

canola oil for deep-frying
16 raw prawns, peeled, de-veined
  and chopped
1 tsp fish sauce
2 tsp chicken stock
½ tsp soy sauce
salt and freshly gound black pepper
4 dumpling wrappers
egg white for sealing

Chicken feet

4 chicken feet, nails removed
5 tbsp golden syrup
2 cups chicken stock
2 tbsp finely chopped ginger
2 tbsp finely chopped garlic
2 tbsp soy sauce

Prawn dumplings

1 Heat the oil in a deep fryer to 180°C.

2 To make the filling, place half the chopped prawns in a food processor and mince, or chop very finely. Place in a bowl with the rest of the chopped prawn meat. Add the fish sauce, chicken stock, soy sauce, and salt and pepper and combine.

3 To make the dumplings, place the filling in the middle of a wrapper. Brush the edges of the wrapper with egg white, fold in half and crimp the edges together. Repeat with the remaining filling and wrappers.

4 Bring a saucepan of water to the boil and top with a tight-fitting bamboo steamer. Place the dumplings in the steamer and steam for 5 minutes or until the wrapper is translucent.

Chicken feet

1 Heat a frying pan to a medium heat and sauté the chicken feet in golden syrup for 7 minutes.

2 Put the stock, ginger, garlic and soy sauce in a saucepan and bring to the boil. Add the chicken feet and simmer for 2 hours or until tender. The meat should fall away from the bone with very little effort.

To serve, arrange all 4 items on a platter with dipping sauces such as sweet chilli sauce and kecap manis mixed with a dash of fish sauce.

Blueberry and goat's cheese wontons

Recipe by Kelly Young

Makes 6 wontons
Preparation time: 10 minutes
Cooking time: 20 minutes

canola oil for deep-frying
1 punnet blueberries
1 tbsp finely chopped crystallised
    ginger, plus 1 tsp finely sliced
2 tbsp caster sugar
juice of 1 lemon
6 wonton wrappers
3 tbsp goat's cheese
micro-cress for serving

1 Half fill a saucepan with canola oil and heat to 180°C for deep-frying.

2 Place two-thirds of the punnet of blueberries in a saucepan with the finely chopped ginger, sugar and half the lemon juice, and simmer over a medium-low heat for 3 minutes or until the sugar has dissolved. Strain through a sieve, reserving the pulp and the juice. Reserve 6 whole cooked blueberries. Whisk the remaining lemon juice into the pulp.

3 Place the wonton wrappers on a clean floured flat surface and spread a teaspoon of goat's cheese in the centre of each wrapper. Spoon a small amount of pulp on top of the goat's cheese and top with a slice of ginger and a whole blueberry. Brush the wonton edges with water and fold in half, sealing the edges and removing any air. Place your finger in the middle of the wrapper and bring the sides around and join together. Deep-fry the wontons for 2–3 minutes or until golden.

4 To serve, place the micro-cress in 3 piles on a plate. Top each pile with a wonton, spoon over the blueberry juice and scatter with the reserved blueberries.

Some people may see this as an unusual combination, but it works. The creamy flavour of the goat's cheese complements the sweet blueberries, finished off with a lingering taste of light ginger. This is a dish that can be served in many different ways: as a single bite-size hors d'oeuvre that you could have at a cocktail party, as an appetiser or even as a main.

Dégustation

Dégustation is the careful, appreciative tasting of a range of dishes.

The dégustation selection from *MasterChef New Zealand* showcased on the next few pages demonstrates what would be, and has been, typically served at Bracu for dégustation diners.

This group of recipes creates a summer dégustation menu. The emphasis is on light, clean ingredients that are in season in the summer months.

At Bracu, we aim to showcase our finest produce with skilful technique and interesting flavour combinations to take the diner on a journey through the senses.

Dégustation dishes are made in smaller portion sizes than what would be usually served on a regular à la carte menu so each course can be savoured and enjoyed.

I hope you enjoy cooking these recipes as much as the contestants did and as much as the judges enjoyed eating them. Bon appétit.

Adrian Brett-Chinnery, Head Chef, Bracu

Tomato consommé

Serves 4
Preparation time: 20 minutes
Cooking time: 1 hour

2 shallots, sliced
¼ cup olive oil
3 cups vine ripened tomatoes,
   roughly chopped
2 cloves garlic, chopped
1 tsp sugar
2 tsp salt
4 cups water
4 egg whites
freshly ground black pepper
2 medium tomatoes
8 asparagus tips, blanched
¼ cup fresh micro-basil leaves

1 To make the broth, heat a frying pan over a medium heat and sweat the shallots in the olive oil until soft. Do not let them colour. Stir in 2 cups of the chopped tomatoes, garlic, sugar and salt, add the water and bring to the boil. Reduce the heat and simmer for 20 minutes, skimming the surface often. Pass through a chinois lined with muslin and chill.

2 Using a stick blender, blend the remaining chopped tomatoes with the egg whites and season with pepper. Put in a saucepan with the broth, whisk together and bring to a slow boil. Reduce to the barest of simmers and cook for 20 minutes. A crust should begin to form on the surface. Break this carefully and ladle the stock through a lined chinois. Repass until the broth is perfectly clear. Chill.

3 To make the tomato concassé, score the top of the whole tomatoes in a criss-cross pattern. Place in a saucepan of salted boiling water and blanch for 20 seconds until the skin just begins to peel off. Remove the tomatoes and refresh in iced water. Remove the skins and cut into quarters. Scoop out the seeds and flesh, and roughly chop.

4 When ready to serve, reheat the soup. Place a teaspoon of the concassé into the bottom of each of 4 demitasse cups, pour in the consommé and top with 2 blanched asparagus tips and fresh basil leaves.

Furikake-seasoned tuna loin with coriander jelly

Serves 8
Preparation time: 20 minutes
Cooking time: 10 minutes plus
  2-3 hours setting time

Tuna
500g yellowfin tuna loin
peanut oil for frying
warmed honey for coating
furikake seasoning for coating

Peanut dressing
20g palm sugar
100ml peanut oil
50ml black vinegar
salt and freshly ground black
  pepper

Coriander jelly
½ pint fish stock
1 tbsp fish sauce
1 tbsp light soy sauce
1 tbsp mirin
2 leaves gelatin, soaked in cold
  water
1 bunch coriander, roughly
  chopped

baby coriander leaves for serving

1 Carefully trim the blood line and sinews off the tuna loin – it should be 300g–400g after trimming. Slice lengthwise into 4 pieces. Roll each piece tightly in clingfilm to form a cylindrical shape and place in the fridge for 1 hour to set.

2 Remove from the fridge, take off the clingfilm and sear the tuna for 1–2 minutes on all sides in a very hot pan with the peanut oil. Brush a little warm honey over the loin to help the seasoning stick. Roll in the furikake seasoning, wrap again in clingfilm and chill in the freezer for half an hour.

3 To make the peanut dressing, finely grate the palm sugar with a microplane into a bowl. Add the remaining ingredients and mix well. Set aside.

4 To make the coriander jelly, heat the fish stock, fish sauce, soy sauce and mirin in a pan over a medium heat. Squeeze out the gelatin and mix into the hot stock. Remove from the heat and leave to cool for 20 minutes. Add in the coriander and check the seasoning. Pour the mixture into 8 moulds to a depth of 2cm. Chill in the fridge for 2–3 hours to set.

5 Slice the tuna into 1cm thick slices. Arrange 3 on each plate with a jelly and garnish with the baby coriander leaves.

Sautéed scampi and smoked duck

Serves 4
Preparation time: 20 minutes
Cooking time: 1½ hours

Beetroot
8 baby beetroot, topped and tailed
  and skin on
3 cloves
2 cardamom pods
1 star anise
½ cinnamon stick
6 black peppercorns
1 tsp coriander seeds

Smoked duck
100g salt
100g soft brown sugar
1 tsp vanilla paste
2 duck breasts, trimmed
½ cup manuka dust
½ cup mixed tea leaves (such as
  jasmine)

Orange and almond foam
200g sliced almonds
350ml water
zest and juice of 1 orange
100ml milk
1 tbsp butter, plus extra for frying
salt to taste
8 scampi tails, shells removed
oil for frying

herb flowers (such as rocket
  flowers) for serving

1 Preheat the oven to 180°C.

2 Place the beetroot in a pan with the spices and 100ml water. Cover and bake for around one and a half hours, checking after 1 hour. The beets are ready when the skin begins to peel off. Remove from the pan and leave to cool. The skins should pop off easily.

3 To prepare the duck, combine the salt, sugar and vanilla paste and rub all over the duck breasts. Wrap in clingfilm, place on a tray and refrigerate for half an hour to 'cure'. Gently wash off the cure so you leave the smallest amount behind. Pat dry the breasts and sear skin side down in a hot oiled pan until the fat is fairly crisp.

4 Line a roasting pan with tinfoil and tip in the manuka dust and tea. Place a cake rack on top and lay the duck breasts on it, skin side up. Wrap the pan in tinfoil and place over a low heat for around 10 minutes or until the breasts are medium rare. Remove from the heat and rest. Chill until required.

5 To make the foam, first lightly toast the almonds in a frying pan. Do not allow them to colour too much. Blend the toasted almonds in a blender with the water to make a milk. Strain into a saucepan. Add the orange zest and juice and the milk, and heat gently but do not boil. Remove from the heat and leave to infuse for 10 minutes. Strain again into a clean saucepan, add the butter, season with salt and keep warm.

6 Sauté the scampi tails in a little oil and butter in a frying pan over a high heat for 3–4 minutes.

7 Warm the duck breasts and cut each into 8 slices. Warm beetroot in a pan. Foam the almond and orange milk with a stick blender.

8 To serve, arrange 2 scampi tails and 2 beetroot per plate. Place a slice of duck breast on each scampi tail and top with a spoonful of almond foam and a sprig of herb flowers.

Wattleseed-seasoned ostrich fillet

Serves 4–6 (depending on portion sizes)
Preparation time: 30 minutes
Cooking time: 2 hours to chill cow curd plus 30 minutes

Whipped cow's curd
75ml cream
2 sprigs thyme
1 clove garlic, roughly chopped
200g cow's curd
salt and freshly ground black pepper

Wattleseed-seasoned ostrich
4 ostrich back fillets, trimmed
150g wattleseeds, crushed
canola oil for frying

Praline
300g sugar
100g hazelnuts, peeled

edible flowers for garnish
1 tbsp freeze-dried raspberries for garnish
1 tbsp savoury chocolate (such as Valrhona Xocopili, available from Sabato, Mt Eden, Auckland) for garnish
pomegranate molasses for garnish

1 Preheat the oven to 200°C.

2 To make the whipped curd, warm the cream in a saucepan over a low heat with the thyme and garlic to just below boiling point. Do not boil. Remove from the heat and cool for 10 minutes, allowing the flavours to infuse. Strain the cream, discarding, the garlic and thyme, then pour into the blender. Add the cow's curd and blitz well. Season to taste. Pour into a stainless steel container and chill to set for 1–2 hours.

3 Roll the ostrich fillets in wattleseed and sear for 1–2 minutes on all sides in a medium ovenproof frying pan with the canola oil. Place in the oven for 2–3 minutes; the meat should be still fairly rare. Rest for 5–7 minutes and season the meat by rolling in wattleseed again. Slice each fillet into 4 pieces.

4 To caramelise the sugar for the praline, place the sugar in a pan and set over a medium–high heat. Leave until the sugar begins to go golden. Move the pan around to stir (don't use a spoon). Place the hazelnuts on a silicone baking mat and pour the caramelised sugar over. Leave to cool completely. Blitz in the food processor until the mixture resembles breadcrumbs. Pulse to remove any large clumps of caramelised sugar.

5 Plate and garnish with edible flowers, freeze-dried raspberries, savoury chocolate, pomegranate molasses, praline and quenelles of the whipped cow's curd.

Pork tortellini with date purée

Makes 10
Preparation time: 1 hour (including
  pasta dough)
Cooking time: 45 minutes

Pasta dough
200g Italian tipo '00' flour
30g fine polenta
4 egg yolks
2 eggs
1 tbsp extra-virgin olive oil
½ tsp salt

Cider jus
200ml cider
200ml beef stock
200ml veal stock
splash apple syrup

Pork filling
½ green apple, peeled, cored and
  finely diced
4 sage leaves, chopped
150g minced pork fillet
1 egg white
salt and freshly ground black pepper
50ml cream

Date purée
200g medjool dates, pitted
25g capers
100ml port
100ml water

16 sage leaves, finely sliced
oil for deep-frying

1 To make the pasta dough, place all the ingredients in a food processor and process until the mixture resembles breadcrumbs. Turn out onto a floured surface and knead for 5 minutes until the dough is smooth and elastic. Wrap in clingfilm and chill for half an hour.

2 To make the jus, pour the cider into a saucepan, bring to the boil, then simmer to reduce by two-thirds. Add both stocks and simmer to reduce by half or until the consistency is right. Add the apple syrup and season to taste.

3 To make the filling, mix all the ingredients by hand in a bowl. Remove a piece of the filling and poach in boiling water to cook. Check the seasoning and adjust to taste.

4 Remove the dough from the fridge and roll out evenly, then pass through a pasta machine, starting with the thickest setting and finishing with the second finest. Rest the dough for 5 minutes. To assemble the tortellini, see gorgonzola tortellini recipe on page 246.

5 To make the purée, place all the ingredients in a saucepan. Bring to the boil and simmer for 15 minutes. Pour into a blender and blend to a smooth purée, then strain into a clean saucepan. Place over a low heat and keep warm until needed.

6 Deep-fry the sage leaves until crisp but not burnt. Drain on a paper towel and season. Leave to cool.

7 Bring a saucepan of salted water to the boil and cook the tortellini in batches for 2–3 minutes or until translucent. Drain.

8 Spoon some date purée into the centre of each bowl, top with tortellini and sage leaves, and pour around the jus.

Market fish with saffron risotto

Serves 4
Preparation time: 15 minutes
Cooking time: 45 minutes

12 slices pancetta

Chorizo foam
1 shallot, chopped
1 clove garlic, chopped
butter for frying
300g chorizo, chopped
1 tsp honey
250ml fish stock
250ml cream
2 sprigs thyme
salt and freshly ground black
   pepper

Risotto
200g arborio rice
500ml fish stock
1 large shallot, finely diced
pinch of saffron threads soaked in
   4 tablespoons hot water
3 tbsp olive oil
4 tbsp white wine
100g pre-cooked shrimps
50g butter, diced
2 tbsp grated Parmesan

4 x 100g–120g fish fillets, skin on
butter or oil for frying
4 clams
splash of white wine
pinch of smoked paprika
rocket leaves for serving

1 Preheat the oven to 140°C.

2 Lay pancetta slices on a tray lined with baking paper. Cover again with baking paper and lay another tray on top to keep them flat. Bake in the oven for 20 minutes, checking after 10 minutes. Remove from the oven and leave to cool. The pancetta will crisp up as it cools.

3 To make the foam, sauté the shallot and garlic in butter in a frying pan over a medium heat. Add the chorizo and brown well, but take care not to burn it. Stir in the honey. Add the fish stock, cream and thyme and bring to a simmer. Remove from the heat and let the mixture infuse for 10 minutes. Strain into a clean saucepan. Season to taste and leave over a low heat to keep warm until needed. When ready to serve, use a stick blender to create the foam.

4 To make the risotto, blanch the rice in boiling salted water for 5 minutes. Drain and chill until cold.

5 Heat the stock in a saucepan and leave simmering on the stovetop.

6 Heat a frying pan over a medium heat and sweat the shallot with the saffron water in the olive oil until soft. Stir in the rice and continue to stir for around 2 minutes. Pour in the white wine and reduce right down. Add ⅓ of the stock and stir, allowing the rice to absorb it. Add another ⅓ of the stock and allow to absorb again. Then add the shrimps. Check the rice; if it is not cooked add more stock. Once the rice is cooked, stir in the butter and Parmesan, and season to taste.

7 Heat a frying pan to high using a little oil, and place the snapper skin side down and cook until golden and crisp. Press down with the fish slice so the fillet cooks evenly. Turn and cook for a further 1–2 minutes (add a knob of butter if desired).

8 Place the clams in a saucepan and pour in the wine. Cover and place over a high heat for 2–3 minutes until the clams have steamed open. Discard any clams that haven't opened.

9 Divide the risotto between 4 plates, top each portion with a fillet of fish, some chorizo foam and a pinch of paprika, then a clam and 8 pancetta wafers.

Lamb saddle

Serves 4
Preparation time: 15 minutes
Cooking time: 1 hour

1 1kg lamb saddle, bone in and
  flaps on
1 200g black pudding, skin
  removed and meat crumbled

Jus Niçois
300ml beef stock
300ml veal stock
2 anchovy fillets, roughly chopped
1 courgette, quartered, de-seeded
  and green part only cut into
  small dice
small handful basil leaves
8 green beans, blanched and each
  cut into 3 pieces
4 semi-dried tomatoes, julienned
8 caperberries, cut in half
1 tbsp dried black olives

Polenta
500ml milk
50g butter
100g polenta (instant)

2 good handfuls spinach

1 Remove the skin from the saddle. Remove the bone carefully and set aside. Tenderise the flap of fat if it is thick with a tenderising hammer. Trim the back flap if there is too much of it. Cut down the middle of the saddle in between the loins so that you have 2 loins with the flap still on. Press the black pudding onto both loins. Roll up and tie with string. Refrigerate to set for 1 hour.

2 To make the jus, pour both stocks into a saucepan and add the anchovies. Bring to the boil and simmer to reduce by half. Pass through a strainer into a clean saucepan. Add the courgette, simmer for 1 minute, then remove the courgette and set aside. Put the jus over a low heat to keep warm but not for too long. Check the seasoning just before serving. Keep the remaining ingredients to one side for garnish.

3 Preheat the oven to 180°C.

4 Season the lamb well all over. Heat an oiled ovenproof frying pan to a high heat and sear the lamb until lightly browned on all sides. Roast in the oven for around 15 minutes or until medium rare, turning after 8 minutes and checking how cooked it is. Remove from the oven and rest for 6–8 minutes. Remove the string and slice each saddle into 4 pieces.

5 To make the polenta, warm the milk and butter in a saucepan over a medium heat. Add the polenta and stir occasionally over the heat for 10–15 minutes. Cover the polenta with a piece of greased baking paper and keep warm.

6 Wilt the spinach in a saucepan over a medium heat with a little butter and salt and pepper. Drain well on a tea towel.

7 Spoon the polenta into the centre of each plate, top with wilted spinach, then a slice of lamb. Add the basil leaves, beans, semi-dried tomatoes, caperberries, olives and courgettes. Spoon the jus over before serving.

Blue cheese dish

Makes 10 brioches
Preparation time: 20 minutes
Cooking time: 1 hour

Brioche
24g fresh yeast
2 tbsp warm milk
500g plain flour
1 tsp salt
2 tbsp caster sugar
6 eggs, beaten
240g butter, softened
1 egg, beaten

Pear relish
good pinch of five-spice
200ml sugar syrup (equal amounts
   of sugar and water boiled
   together and cooled; extra syrup
   can be stored in the fridge for up
   to a month)
2 pears, peeled and diced finely
pinch of salt

30g blue cheese per person, at
   room temperature

1 To make the brioche, add the yeast to the warm milk and mix to a paste. Place the flour, salt and sugar in a food processor and mix well. Mix the eggs in with the yeast. With the mixer on low speed, gradually add the egg mix to the dry ingredients and mix until smooth. With mixer still on low, add the butter a little at a time until fully incorporated.

2 Divide the dough into 50g balls and place each in a lined mini-loaf pan. Cover with greased clingfilm and leave in a warm place until doubled in size (about 30 minutes).

3 Mix the five-spice into the sugar syrup and place in a pan. Bring to a simmer and add the pears. Simmer until the pears are just beginning to become soft and a knife can just cut through them easily. Leave to cool in the syrup. Season with a small amount of salt. Chill.

4 Preheat the oven to 180°C.

5 Glaze the tops of the brioche with beaten egg and bake for 10–15 minutes. Place on a wire rack to cool.

6 Serve with a portion of blue cheese and a quenelle of pear relish.

Iced nougatine parfait

Makes 10 parfaits
Preparation time: Overnight to
 freeze parfait plus 20 minutes
Cooking time: 3 hours to chill
 mousse plus 30 minutes

Parfait
150ml egg whites
75g liquid honey
125g caster sugar
200g praline, blitzed in food
 processor (see recipe p 107)
600ml semi-whipped cream

Milk chocolate mousse
335ml cream
1 leaf gelatin, soaked in cold water
335g milk chocolate
500ml cream, semi-whipped

Strawberry juice
1kg frozen strawberries
50ml sugar syrup (see page 111)
juice of ½ lemon

Praline tuile
300g sugar
100g peeled and roasted hazelnuts

sprigs mint for garnish
fresh strawberries for garnish

1 Partly whisk the egg whites in the cake mixer. Place the honey and sugar in a saucepan and bring to the boil. While continuing to whisk the whites, slowly pour in the honey mixture. This will make an Italian meringue. Continue to whisk until cool.

2 Fold the praline into the semi-whipped cream. Carefully fold the meringue into the cream mixture and spoon into 10 65–70ml dariole moulds. Freeze until required.

3 To make the mousse, heat the 335ml cream in a saucepan over a medium heat but do not boil. Remove from heat, add the gelatin and mix. Set aside.

4 Bring a saucepan of water to the boil, then reduce to a simmer. In a metal bowl that fits snugly over the saucepan, melt the chocolate. Add the melted chocolate to the cream and gelatin mixture and combine well. Leave to cool to room temperature.

5 Gently fold the semi-whipped cream into the chocolate mixture. Transfer to a stainless steel container and blast chill (or chill in the fridge for 3 hours).

6 To make the strawberry juice, place the strawberries in a metal bowl and cover tightly with clingfilm. Place the bowl over a saucepan of simmering water for about an hour or until all the juice has bled from the strawberries. Strain the juice through muslin into a clean saucepan and bring to the boil. Lower the heat and simmer to reduce by one-third, then add sugar syrup and lemon juice. Chill until needed.

7 To caramelise the sugar for the praline, place the sugar in a pan and set over a medium–high heat. Leave until the sugar begins to go golden. Move the pan around to stir; don't use a spoon. Place the hazelnuts on a silicone baking mat, pour the caramelised sugar over and leave to cool completely. Blitz in the food processor until the mixture resembles breadcrumbs and pass through a sieve.

8 Preheat the oven to 180°C.

9 Spread over a tuile mould on a silicone baking mat and bake for 3 minutes or until golden. Leave to cool on the baking mat, then carefully remove.

10 Dip the moulds into boiling water for about 2 seconds to loosen, then tip onto plate.

11 For each portion serve a slice of parfait, a quenelle of mousse, a praline tuile, garnish with fresh strawberries and mint sprigs, and fill shot glasses with the chilled strawberry juice.

Hot lemon soufflé

Makes 8 soufflés
Preparation time: 30 minutes
Cooking time: 10 minutes

Lemon gelato
250ml lemon juice
250ml sugar syrup, cooled
250ml milk

Lemon syrup
250ml sugar syrup (see page 111)
zest and juice of 2 lemons
1 vanilla pod, split

Lemon sabayon base
9 egg yolks
255g caster sugar
300ml fresh lemon juice

Meringue
6 egg whites
6 tbsp caster sugar
icing sugar for serving

icing sugar for dusting

1 Preheat the oven to 190°C.

2 To make the gelato, whisk together all the ingredients. Freeze in Pacojet container. Pacojet and freeze again until needed. (Alternatively, use an ice-cream churner and follow manufacturer's instructions.)

3 To make the lemon syrup, place all the ingredients in a saucepan over a medium heat for around 5 minutes to infuse the pod. Remove the pod and set the syrup aside.

4 To make the sabayon, whisk the egg yolks and sugar in a food processor until the yolks become pale and airy. Pour the lemon juice into a saucepan, place over a high heat and bring to the boil. With the processor whisking on medium speed, slowy pour the hot juice into the eggs. Turn up to full power and whisk until cooled. Refrigerate until required.

5 To make the meringue, whisk the egg whites until soft peaks form that hold when you turn the bowl upside down. Gradually stir in the caster sugar.

6 Place 4 tablespoons of sabayon in a metal bowl. Add 3 tablespoons of meringue and mix well. Gently fold in the rest of whites. Heap into 8 buttered ramekins and smooth the tops. Bake for 6–7 minutes in the lower half of the oven or until risen and golden on top.

7 Dust the soufflés with icing sugar and serve immediately with the lemon gelato on the side and the lemon syrup in a small jug.

Mains

Larb gai

Recipe by Brett McGregor
Serves 4
Preparation time: 20 minutes
Cooking time: 20 minutes

4 tbsp long-grain rice
2 skinless and boneless chicken
  breasts, finely chopped
3 chicken thighs, trimmed of fat
  and finely chopped by hand
8 kaffir lime leaves, finely sliced
2½ dried red chillies, ground
juice of 2 lemons
juice of 4 limes
2 shallots, finely sliced
1 red onion, finely diced
4 tbsp fish sauce
1 cup roughly chopped mint leaves
1 cup roughly chopped coriander
  leaves
1 cucumber, peeled, de-seeded and
  finely sliced for serving
2 red chillies, finely sliced
  lengthwise

1 Heat a dry frying pan over a medium heat. Add the rice and toast until golden, tossing to brown the grains evenly. Cool, then grind the rice to a fine powder in a mortar and pestle. Set aside.

2 Place the chicken breasts and thighs in a saucepan and just cover with water. Put the pan over a low heat and gently bring to a simmer. Continue simmering until the chicken is just cooked, then add the lime leaves, dried chilli, lemon and lime juice, shallots, red onion and fish sauce. Stir through the mint and coriander leaves and ground rice.

3 Arrange the cucumber slices in the bottom of a serving bowl, top with the larb and sprinkle with sliced fresh chilli.

This dish instantly transports me to Thailand. I've travelled through Asia many times and this would have to be one of the standout dishes for me. It's simple, delicious and really sums up Thai cuisine nicely. I first sampled larb on the beach in southern Thailand. It was a hot day and I wanted something with a bit of zing that was fresh and clean tasting — I was so surprised at just how much taste was packed into such a small plate. I decided to try to learn the dish from a local, and did. The trickiest part is toasting the rice to give a lovely crunch.

Creamy chicken fricassée and orange kumara scone with asparagus, lemon butter and cashews

I used a tried-and-tested, well-loved original fricassée recipe for my MasterChef audition dish. Over the years, when I have made this dish, I usually boil a chicken and add it to a vegetable and cream sauce. My challenge for the audition was to produce it in 1 hour. I got the idea for the kumara scone topping from my daughter-in-law. This was a totally new idea to me and I was delighted with how an orange-coloured kumara with a little gruyère cheese could add such charm to a humble dish. The homemade chicken stock seems to be the hidden answer to imparting such a rich taste to the fricassée. I love the exquisite taste of fresh French tarragon, too, but you have to use the right amount so that it's not overpowering. This dish is a must for every New Zealand family — the children will love it.

Recipe by Sue Drummond
Serves 4
Preparation time: 30 minutes
Cooking time: 1¾ hours

1 medium orange kumara, unpeeled
5 chicken thighs, bone in
50g butter
3 carrots, peeled and sliced (reserve the skins)
1 onion, chopped (reserve the ends)
1 leek (white part only), sliced (reserve the ends)
1 stick celery, sliced and leaves chopped
2 cloves garlic, chopped
small handful thyme leaves, chopped
2 sprigs rosemary
1 tbsp chopped fresh tarragon
1 large bay leaf
1 tbsp cornflour
1 heaped tsp powdered mustard
⅔ cup milk
salt and freshly ground black pepper

1 Preheat the oven to 200°C.

2 Place the kumara on an oven tray and bake until tender. Peel and mash.

3 De-bone and trim the chicken thighs. Cut meat into chunky pieces and set aside for fricassée. Set aside bones and trim for the stock.

4 To make the stock, place the bones and trim in a saucepan over a medium heat. Add half the butter and cook until the bones are browned, turning occasionally. Add the reserved carrot skins, onion ends, leek ends, celery, garlic, and half the thyme, rosemary, and tarragon. Brown well. Pour in 2 cups water and simmer for 40–50 minutes. Strain the stock into a bowl and set aside.

5 To make the fricassée, heat a saucepan over a medium heat and brown the chicken pieces in the reserved butter, turning occasionally. Add the carrot, onion and leek and cook until the vegetables are soft. Then add 1 cup of the stock, remaining tarragon, rosemary and thyme and the bay leaf and simmer for 10–15 minutes.

6 Combine the cornflour and mustard in a bowl. Pour in a bit of strained stock and the milk, and mix well. Add to the fricassée and season with salt and pepper. Simmer for a further 10–15 minutes.

(continued overleaf)

Kumara scone

1 cup plain flour, extra for dusting
2 tsp baking powder
25g butter
½ cup grated gruyère cheese
¼ cup chopped parsley
⅓ cup milk
1 egg yolk, beaten

Lemon butter

juice of ½ lemon
juice of ½ lime
1 tsp honey
50g butter
1 tbsp flour

20 asparagus spears, stalk ends
  trimmed
½ cup cashews, roasted and
  chopped

7 To make the scone, place the flour and baking powder in a bowl. Rub in the butter. Add the reserved kumara, gruyère and parsley, and mix in enough milk to make a soft dough. Lightly flour a flat surface and turn out the dough. Gently roll out to a rectangle, about 20cm x 10cm and 1cm thick and cut into rectangles or rounds.

8 Transfer the fricassée to a deep casserole dish and place the scone shapes on top. Brush with the egg yolk and bake for 20 minutes or until the scone is cooked.

9 To make the lemon butter sauce, place a saucepan over a medium heat. Heat the lemon and lime juices and honey. Then whisk in the butter and flour. Skim off the froth.

10 Bring a saucepan of water to the boil. Place the asparagus in a steamer that fits tightly over the pan and steam for 2–3 minutes or until the asparagus is tender.

11 Serve the fricassée with the asparagus on the side. Spoon the sauce over the asparagus and scatter with the cashew nuts.

Citrus and herb stuffed chicken breast with caramelised shallots, apple and white wine sauce

Recipe by Mark Harvey
Serves 4
Preparation time: 15 minutes
Cooking time: 30 minutes

4 tbsp finely chopped thyme leaves
4 tbsp finely chopped flat-leaf
  parsley
grated zest of 1 lemon
100g butter, softened
4 boned chicken breasts, skin on
salt and freshly ground black pepper
10 shallots, peeled and halved
2 apples, peeled, cored and cut into
  small wedges
drizzle of extra-virgin olive oil
1½ cup white wine
1½ cup chicken stock
4 tbsp brown sugar
2 small handfuls snow peas for
  serving
1 apple, peeled, cored and julienned
  for serving

1 Preheat the oven to 180°C.

2 To make the herb butter, combine the thyme, parsley, lemon zest and butter in a small bowl. Make a pocket between the chicken skin and flesh, and spoon in the butter. Season with salt and pepper.

3 Heat an oiled ovenproof frying pan over a medium heat. Place the chicken breasts in the pan skin side down and cook for 3–5 minutes or until golden. Add the shallots and apple, and a drizzle of extra-virgin olive oil. Turn the chicken over and place in the oven for 10–12 minutes or until cooked, turning the shallots and apple occasionally during cooking. Remove the chicken and rest for 5 minutes. Slice each breast on the diagonal into thick slices.

4 Place the pan back over a medium heat, add the white wine and cook for a further few minutes. Then add the stock and sugar, and simmer until the sauce has reduced and the apple and shallots have caramelised. Season to taste.

5 Bring a saucepan of salted water to the boil, then reduce to a simmer. Blanch the snow peas for 2–3 minutes and drain.

6 Place the caramelised apple and shallots to the side of a serving plate and arrange the chicken around it. Top with julienned apple and spoon the sauce over. Serve the snow peas in a dish on the side.

I love mixing meat with fruit. This is a quick, easy dish that looks good and tastes great. I must admit it was a bit of a gamble using chicken with apples, but the gamble paid off and I made it into the top six with this dish. Make sure you use good-quality free-range chicken breasts if you can find them. If cooked properly, the skin should be crisp, the apples soft and the shallots firm to the bite. If you want a slightly more tart sauce, you can omit the sugar.

Chicken mignon medallions with chicken mousse timbale, roasted cherry tomatoes and potato rösti

This was the first dish I cooked in the MasterChef kitchen and I was really happy with the way it turned out. I wanted to highlight the versatility of chicken by serving it two ways, while creating a dish full of contrast and balance. Lightly roasting the tomatoes helps to bring out their natural sugars, which complements the salty bacon well. Adding a crisp potato rösti balances the soft, creamy texture of the mousse. The judges said that this was a great looking dish — a little edible garnish goes a long way!

Recipe by Kirsty Cardy
Serves 4
Preparation time: 30 minutes
Cooking time: 30 minutes

Garlic butter
2 cloves garlic, crushed
100g unsalted butter, softened to
   room temperature
2 large basil leaves, finely sliced

Chicken mignon medallions
4 skinless and boneless chicken
   thighs
freshly ground black pepper
8 strips streaky bacon

Chicken mousse timbale
reserved chicken trimmings
2 egg whites
150ml cream
salt and freshly ground black pepper
2 large courgettes, thinly sliced
   lengthwise

Roasted tomatoes
½ punnet cherry tomatoes
salt and freshly ground black pepper
olive oil for drizzling

Rösti
1 floury potato
salt and freshly ground black pepper

1 To make the garlic butter, heat a frying pan over a medium heat and sauté the garlic in a little of the butter. Allow garlic to cool slightly, then fold through the remaining softened butter. Add half the basil and mix to combine. Place butter on clingfilm and roll into a cylinder. Place in the fridge until ready to serve.

2 To make the mignon medallions, sprinkle each chicken thigh with pepper. Roll up each thigh and then wrap in bacon. Secure with kitchen string. Trim excess meat off the ends to form even 'tubes' and reserve the trimmed meat. Allow mignons to set in fridge for 20 minutes.

3 Preheat the oven to 175°C.

4 Brown the mignons in an oiled ovenproof frying pan over a medium heat. Place in the oven and cook for 20 minutes.

5 To make the timbale, mince the reserved chicken trimmings in a food processor. Add the egg whites one at a time. While the motor is still running, pour in the cream, then add the remaining basil. Season with salt and pepper.

6 Grease 4 ramekins with oil and line with strips of courgette, laid out in a star shape. Fill with the chicken-mousse mixture and bake for 25 minutes.

7 Season the tomatoes with salt, pepper and olive oil. Place on an oven tray and bake for 5 minutes until just soft.

8 To make the rösti, grate the potato into a tea towel and squeeze out all the moisture. Season with salt and pepper. Heat an oiled frying pan to high and drop tablespoons of potato into the pan. Flatten to around 1cm thick and fry until golden on both sides.

9 To serve, slice the mignons in half on an angle. Place 2 halves on each plate and top with garlic butter. Invert a timbale onto each plate and place tomatoes alongside. Finish with a rösti cut in half.

Chicken parcel surprise with red wine sauce and broccoli purée

Simon said, 'I love your work'. Ray said, 'I'd pay for it. It's lip-smacking good!' These comments brought tears of happiness to my eyes. It's such a great feeling to have professionals compliment your food. I had played around with de-boning a chicken once before this challenge with the help of a cookbook. Since the show, I have learnt a quicker and easier way of doing it.

Recipe by Kelly Young
Serves 4
Preparation time: 25–30 minutes
Cooking time: 30 minutes

Chicken parcels
4 whole chicken legs, skin on and
　bone in
1 chicken breast, chopped
10 button mushrooms, roughly
　chopped
2 shallots, finely diced
salt and freshly ground black
　pepper
¼ cup pine nuts, toasted
1 tsp Dijon mustard
olive oil for drizzling

Red wine sauce
½ cup red wine
1 cup chicken stock
2 tbsp balsamic vinegar
1 tbsp butter
2 tbsp finely chopped thyme leaves

Broccoli purée
1½ cups chicken stock
2 cups chopped broccoli
2 shallots, finely diced

1 De-bone the chicken legs and set aside.

2 To make the stuffing, mince the chopped chicken breast in a food processor and transfer to a bowl. Heat an oiled frying pan over a medium heat and sauté the mushrooms and shallots until soft. Season with salt and pepper. Place in the bowl with the minced chicken, add the pine nuts and Dijon mustard and combine.

3 Spread a quarter of the stuffing on the inside each boned leg and roll into a ball. Season with salt and pepper. Wrap the balls tightly in clingfilm and then in tinfoil. Place in a saucepan of water over a medium heat and bring to the boil. Reduce to a simmer and simmer for 15 minutes. Remove and rest for 5 minutes.

4 Preheat the oven to 180°C.

5 Unwrap the parcels and place on an oven tray. Drizzle with olive oil and bake for 12–15 minutes or until browned and cooked. Rest for 5 minutes.

6 To make the red wine sauce, pour the wine, stock and vinegar into a saucepan placed over a medium heat. Simmer until the liquid is reduced by three-quarters. Add the butter and thyme leaves, whisking to combine, and cook a further few minutes. Season with salt and pepper.

7 To make the broccoli purée, pour the stock into a saucepan placed over a medium heat. Add the broccoli and shallots and simmer for 8–10 minutes or until the vegetables are soft. Transfer to a blender with enough liquid to blend to a chunky purée. Season with salt and pepper.

8 Slice each chicken parcel into thirds. To serve, drizzle red wine sauce onto each serving plate, arrange the chicken slices on top and spoon the broccoli purée on the side.

Stuffed chicken breasts with cumin-scented carrot purée and spinach cream

At first glance this recipe looks a bit tricky, but if you just do one step at a time I'm sure you will be pleased with the results. My herb of choice for the mousse is tarragon, but when I cooked this in the MasterChef chicken challenge, there wasn't any available so I used basil instead. Try to get fresh tarragon, as the subtle aniseed flavor is superb with chicken. Watercress is a really good substitute for the spinach in the sauce and would provide a nice peppery taste. Visually, this is a great dish and, I assure you, it tastes even better than it looks!

Recipe by Tracey Gunn
Serves 2
Preparation time: 20 minutes
Cooking time: 40 minutes

2 boned chicken breasts, skin on

Chicken mousse
2 skinless and boneless chicken
  thighs
salt and freshly ground black pepper
1 egg white
handful chopped basil
100ml cream

Carrot purée
50g butter
½ tsp ground cumin
3 large carrots, peeled and chopped
100ml cream

Spinach cream
400ml vegetable stock
400ml cream
1 clove garlic, chopped
1tsp cornflour
½ tsp nutmeg
2 handfuls spinach leaves

1 bunch baby carrots, tops trimmed

1 To make the mousse, remove the tenderloins from underneath the chicken breasts. Blend in a food processor with the thigh meat until coarsely chopped. Season with salt and pepper, and blend again until minced. Add the egg white and basil, and process until smooth. Then pour in the cream while the motor is running until combined.

2 Lift the skin from the chicken breasts, and spoon the mousse into the pocket. Roll the breasts into a sausage shape. Wrap in clingfilm and tie with string. Poach in a saucepan of almost boiling water over a medium heat for 12 minutes. Remove and rest for 10 minutes.

3 Preheat the oven to 200°C.

4 Remove the clingfilm and tie the breasts to retain their sausage shape. Brown the chicken in butter and oil in an ovenproof frying pan over a medium heat. Then bake in the oven for 10 minutes. Rest again for 8–10 minutes.

5 To make the carrot purée, melt the butter in a saucepan over a medium heat. Add the cumin and cook for 1 minute. Add the carrots and season with salt and pepper. Pour in the cream and cook until the carrots are tender. Transfer to a blender and blend until smooth, then sieve to make a really smooth purée.

6 To make the spinach cream, bring the stock, cream and garlic to the boil in a saucepan over a medium-high heat. Mix the cornflour with a bit of water and stir into the stock. Remove from the heat and add the nutmeg and spinach, and season with salt and pepper. Transfer to a blender and blend until the cream is very smooth and bright green. Adjust the seasoning to taste.

(continued overleaf)

7 Bring a saucepan of lightly salted water to the boil. Boil the baby carrots for 3–4 minutes or until tender. Remove and drain.

8 To serve, spread the carrot purée on one side of each plate. Cut each breast on the diagonal into around 5 pieces and arrange on the purée. Pour a line of spinach cream down the middle and place baby carrots on the opposite side to the chicken.

Chicken with garlic and sage cream sauce

This dish is a slight adaptation of something my mother taught me when I was a teenager. You may remember my little mistake during the show when I ran off into the pantry to grab what I thought I needed, but unfortunately for me, I forgot to count the ingredients I was grabbing and throwing onto the wooden tray. Confidently, I left the pantry and began the walk back to my station. Counting on the way revealed a terrible mistake — I had 12 ingredients, not 10! I was left with a very uncomfortable wait until I could reveal the problem — I thought it would send me home. Luckily, Ross decided to take some ingredients from my tray as punishment (not the ones I wanted him to take) and told me to get creative. So, lots of garlic, sage leaves, chicken stock and cream created a very delicious dish. You can also fry some sage leaves to use as garnish at the end. Delicious.

Recipe by Brett McGregor

Serves 4
Preparation time: 25 minutes
Cooking time: 35 minutes

2 tbsp oil
4 skinless and boneless chicken
   breasts
30g butter
2 shallots, finely chopped
2 cloves garlic, finely chopped
10 sage leaves
½ cup chicken stock
½ cup cream
salt and freshly ground black
   pepper
8 green beans, trimmed and sliced
   lengthwise

1 Preheat the oven to 180°C.

2 Heat the oil in an ovenproof frying pan over a medium heat. Brown the chicken on both sides, then place the pan in the oven for 10–15 minutes until the chicken is cooked, depending on the thickness of the breasts. Rest for 5 minutes. Slice each breast into 4 pieces.

3 To make the sauce, melt the butter in a frying pan. Add the shallots, garlic and sage leaves, and cook until the garlic is golden. Add the stock and simmer to reduce by half, then pour in the cream and cook until the sauce is thick enough to coat the back of a spoon. Season with salt and pepper to taste.

4 Bring a saucepan of salted water to the boil and cook the beans until tender. Drain and toss with a knob of butter and season with salt and pepper.

5 To serve, place a sliced chicken breast in centre of each plate and spoon around the sauce. Arrange the sliced beans on top.

Note: To add flavour to the sauce you can use the cooking juices from the chicken. Once the chicken breasts are cooked, remove from the pan. Place the pan on the stovetop on a high heat and pour in ¼ cup of chicken stock. Bring to the boil, scraping up the sticky browned bits on the bottom of the pan. This concentrated flavour of the juices can be

Portuguese chicken thighs with melon, capsicum, mint and lime salsa

Recipe by Nigel Anderson
Serves 2
Preparation time: 20 minutes
Cooking time: 30 minutes

2 red capsicums
2 tbsp roughly chopped fresh
  oregano
4 cloves garlic
1 red chilli, de-seeded and chopped
1 tsp smoked paprika
1 tsp ground cumin
2 tbsp extra-virgin olive oil
zest and juice of 2 limes
1 pepperdew pepper
salt to taste
4 chicken thighs, bone in and skin on
1 cup chicken stock
2 limes for garnish, sliced in half

Salsa
½ rockmelon, peeled, de-seeded
  and finely diced
2 green capsicum, cored and finely
  diced
bunch of mint, chopped
grated zest and juice of 1 lime

lime wedges for serving

1 Heat an oven grill or barbecue to hot.

2 Chargrill the capsicums until the skin blisters and blackens. Remove the capsicums and change the oven setting to bake and preheat to 180°C. Place the capsicums in a plastic bag for 10 minutes, then remove the skins. Core and roughly chop, then place in a food processor with the oregano, garlic, chilli, paprika, cumin, oil, lime zest and juice, and pepperdew and process to a fine consistency. Season with salt.

3 Heat a frying pan over a medium heat and add the sauce. Simmer until the sauce reduces to a thick paste.

4 Place the chicken skin side down on a hot chargrill pan and brown until the skin is golden. Spoon some paste on the side facing up, then put the pan in the oven for 10 minutes. Turn the chicken and spoon more paste onto the skin side. Return to the oven for a further 15 minutes.

5 Place the pan with the chicken still in it back over a medium heat and pour in the stock. Reduce to a sauce consistency.

6 To make the salsa, place the rockmelon and capsicum in a bowl. Add the mint and lime zest and juice, and combine.

7 To serve, place the thighs on plates and spoon over the sauce. Put the salsa in a side dish and finish with lime wedges.

I made this dish for one of the mystery box challenges. My game plan for any chicken challenge that might present itself was to go with a reasonably simple cooking method and create big flavours. I've always enjoyed a little heat in a dish and find this, coupled with some citrus, to be a winning combination. I think the capsicum marinade is original enough to be very interesting. This dish was paired with a fresh salsa, made with capsicum, rockmelon, lime and mint.

Quick chicken curry on spiced potato cakes with fried bread and yoghurt

Recipe by Robert Trathen
Serves 2
Preparation time: 10 minutes
Cooking time: 30 minutes

Potato cake
2 large potatoes, peeled and cut
  into chunks
oil for frying
½ tbsp cumin seeds, toasted
salt to taste

Chicken curry
1 tbsp garlic, crushed
1 tbsp ginger, crushed
300g boneless and skinless chicken
  thighs, trimmed and cut into 4cm
  pieces
2 tsp turmeric
¾ cup yoghurt, plus extra for serving
½ cup roughly chopped fresh
  coriander leaves, plus extra for
  serving
salt to taste

Bread
½ cup self-raising flour, sifted
1 cup plain flour, sifted
½ tsp salt
1 tbsp cumin seeds
¾ cup warm water
canola oil for frying

1 To make the potato cakes, place the chopped potato in a saucepan of lightly salted water and bring to the boil. Cook until just tender, then drain well.

2 Heat a frying pan to medium and drizzle with oil. Add the potatoes and cumin seeds and fry until golden. Squash the potato into a cookie cutter to make a cake, then repeat to make the second cake.

3 To make the chicken curry, heat a saucepan to medium and gently fry the garlic and ginger in a little oil until soft. Set aside.

4 Coat the chicken pieces in turmeric, then place in an oiled frying pan over a medium heat. Brown the chicken all over. Add ½ cup water and the cooked ginger and garlic, and simmer for 7 minutes or until cooked. Remove the chicken from the pan and place in a bowl. Add the yoghurt and coriander, and toss gently to coat the chicken well. Season with salt.

5 To make the bread, mix together the flours, salt and cumin seeds in a large bowl. Add a small drizzle of oil, then the warm water. Mix with your hands, then add some cold water and mix until the dough forms a ball. Wrap in clingfilm and rest for 15 minutes. Then roll out the dough to 4mm thick and cut into 4cm rounds with a cookie cutter.

6 Heat 5cm of oil in a large saucepan to hot. Gently place the dough rounds in the oil and fry until brown and puffy. Remove with a slotted spoon and drain on paper towels.

7 To serve, place a potato cake on each plate and top with the chicken curry. Drizzle with yoghurt and sprinkle with coriander. Serve the bread on the side.

This dish was taught to me by my mother-in-law, Rosalie. She is of Indian heritage and makes the best curries! My partner, Kathleen, also makes beautiful curries so they are a regular dinner for us. This was a very difficult challenge to achieve with only 10 ingredients. I love heat in my curry but had to omit this because I also wanted to impress by making fried bread or puri. Diced cucumber is a great addition to yoghurt to make a raita.

Chicken pot pie

This pie saved my bacon after the 'banoffee shocker' incident. When my banoffee pie turned into a liquid smoothie, my place in the competition hinged on my chicken pot pie — and it came through a winner as 'dish of the day'! I have always enjoyed eating chicken pies, but had never attempted to make one, let alone making the pastry as well. But I knew the flavours and textures I liked, so I set about attempting to replicate those — I wanted a smooth white sauce with beautiful hunks of chicken, the crunch of corn and carrots. This recipe is really very easy. The roux is made with chicken stock, then the other ingredients are simply stirred in. The pastry is made even tastier by the addition of herbs and a sprinkling of poppy seeds on top. Enjoy!

Recipe by Steve Juergens
Serves 4
Preparation time: 1 hour
Cooking time: 25 minutes

shortcrust pastry (recipe on page 44) with 1 tbsp chopped thyme and 1 tbsp chopped rosemary added

1 medium Agria potato, peeled and cut into 1cm chunks
1 cob sweetcorn
butter for frying
2 medium onions, finely chopped
1 clove garlic, finely chopped
1 medium carrot, peeled and finely chopped
1 small leek, finely sliced
100g mushrooms, cut into quarters
100g bacon, diced
3 boneless and skinless chicken thighs, cut into 2cm pieces
oil for frying
50g butter
50g flour
100ml milk
400ml chicken stock

1 Prepare the shortcrust pastry by following the recipe on page 44, adding the chopped thyme and rosemary after the flour. Wrap in clingfilm and refrigerate until required.

2 Place the potato chunks in a saucepan of lightly salted water and boil until just tender. Drain and run under cold water to stop cooking. Drain again and set aside.

3 Boil the corn cob in a saucepan of lightly salted water until just tender. Drain and set aside. When cool, cut the kernels from the cob.

4 Heat a saucepan over a low heat, melt a knob of butter and add the onions, garlic, carrot and leek. Cover and sweat for 5 minutes until the vegetables are soft but not coloured. Set aside.

5 Heat a frying pan over a medium heat and sauté the mushrooms in butter until soft. Set aside.

6 Fry the bacon and chicken in the same pan with a little oil until browned. Set aside.

7 Preheat the oven to 180°C.

8 To make a roux, melt the 50g butter in a saucepan over a low heat, then stir in the flour and cook while continuing to stir. Slowly add the milk, then the chicken stock and wine. Bring to a simmer, stirring constantly. Simmer for 5 minutes.

9 Remove the pan from the heat and add the onion, mushroom and chicken mixtures, then add the parboiled potatoes and sweetcorn kernels. Season with salt and pepper. Mix well and place in an ovenproof dish. Allow to cool for 10 minutes.

10 Roll out the pastry to 5mm thick and cover the top of the dish. Cut a couple of slits in the pastry, brush with the egg yolk and sprinkle with poppy seeds.

11 Bake the pie for 20 minutes or until the pastry is golden brown.

Curried barbecued lamb and kumara pie

Recipe by Sue Drummond
Serves 4
Preparation time: 10–12 hours
Cooking time: 45 minutes

Marinade
1 clove garlic
6cm piece ginger
juice of 3 lemons
2 tsp garam masala
2 tsp ground coriander
2 tsp ground cumin
2 tsp turmeric
1 tsp ground ginger
2 tbsp oil

small boned leg of lamb, cut into
  good-sized chunks
shortcrust pastry (see recipe on
  page 44)
1 medium onion, roughly chopped
1 large kumara, peeled and diced
1 medium carrot, peeled and diced
salt and freshly ground black pepper
1¼ cups beef stock
½ cup milk
2 tablespoons flour
1 egg yolk, beaten

1 Place all the marinade ingredients in a food processor and process to a paste. Coat the lamb well with the marinade and marinate for at least 10 hours.

2 Prepare the pastry, following the recipe on page 44, making a double quantity for a base and lid and blind baking the base. Set the remaining pastry aside for the lid.

3 Heat the oven grill to high and grill the lamb pieces on all sides until browned. Set aside. Change the oven setting to bake and preheat the oven to 180°C.

4 To make the filling, place the onion, kumara and carrot in a saucepan with oil over a medium heat. Cover and sweat the vegetables until soft. Remove the kumara and set aside.

5 Add the grilled lamb to the vegetables, and season with salt and pepper. Pour in the stock and gently add the milk. Stir in the flour to thicken. Simmer for 45 minutes, adding the kumara in the last 15 minutes.

6 Spoon the filling into the prepared pastry base, roll the reserved pastry out to 5mm thick and use to cover the pie, crimping the edges together to seal. Decorate the top with a pastry fern and brush on the beaten egg yolk.

7 Bake in the oven for 20–25 minutes or until the pastry is golden.

The idea for the flavour of the lamb in this pie comes from a long-loved recipe, served and especially remembered from our eldest son's twenty-first birthday party where the lamb was cooked on a round charcoal barbecue. The butterflied leg of lamb was one of the first recipes to inspire my use of coriander, garam masala and cumin, here combined with the lovely lemon and ginger flavours.

Spring lamb backstrap with balsamic glaze and Gargoillou salad

I developed this dish for my MasterChef audition as a way of showing the judges everything I love about cooking on one plate. I always cook with seasonal produce so picked asparagus and lamb (two quintessential spring ingredients). The Gargouillou salad (invented by French chef Michel Bras) is made from lots of different vegetables, seeds and flowers arranged to represent the garden from which they came. What I love about this dish is that, with the exception of the lamb, all the elements are completely interchangeable. You could try coating other vegetables in the crisp crumbs or substituting the salad ingredients for vegetables that are in season, that you like, or have grown yourself.

Recipe by Kirsty Cardy
Serves 2
Preparation time: 1 hour
Cooking time: 40 minutes

Balsamic glaze
2 cloves garlic, finely chopped
1 tbsp butter
½ cup balsamic vinegar
2 tbsp brown sugar

Lamb
2 tbsp fresh rosemary leaves, finely chopped
1 clove garlic, finely chopped
2 lamb backstraps
salt and freshly ground black pepper

Gargouillou salad
5 baby potatoes
4 asparagus spears
1 egg, lightly beaten
¼ cup rice bubbles, crushed
oil for frying
handful flat-leaf parsley
Parmesan cheese, shaved
1 courgette, sliced into 5mm-thick rounds

1 Preheat the oven to 180°C.

2 To make the glaze, heat a frying pan over a medium heat and sauté the garlic in the butter until soft. Add the vinegar and brown sugar, turn down the heat and simmer to reduce the liquid by one-third. Set aside.

3 Combine the rosemary and garlic in a small bowl. Season the lamb backstraps with salt and pepper, brush with the balsamic glaze, then roll in the rosemary and garlic mixture. Set aside.

4 To make the Gargoillou salad, first parboil the potatoes. Bring a saucepan of salted water to the boil, then reduce to a simmer, add the potatoes and cook until tender, drain and set aside. Coat the asparagus in the beaten egg, then coat in the rice bubbles. Heat enough oil in a frying pan over a medium heat to shallow-fry the asparagus. Fry the asparagus until golden. Drain on paper towels and set aside. Cut the potatoes in half and place a parsley leaf and piece of shaved Parmesan in the centre of each half. Then, using the same frying pan, fry both sides until golden. Set aside. Again in the same pan, place in the courgette rounds, topped with a shave of Parmesan, and cook until the bottom of the courgette is golden and the cheese has begun to melt. Sauté the mushrooms in butter and set aside. Cut grooves down the length of the carrots and then cut into rings; they should look like tiny flowers.

5 To make the asparagus purée, heat a frying pan over a medium heat, add the butter and sauté the garlic, onion and asparagus. Add vegetable stock and cook until tender. Season with salt and freshly ground black pepper. Place in a food processor and process until smooth.

(continued overleaf)

4 button mushrooms, finely sliced
butter for frying
2 baby carrots

Asparagus purée
30g butter
1 clove garlic
¼ onion, sliced
1 bunch asparagus, trimmed
¼ cup vegetable stock

Beetroot purée and vinaigrette
½ cup white balsamic vinegar
1 large beetroot, peeled and cubed
4 whole cloves
pinch of sugar
⅓ cup olive oil

¼ cup micro-greens for serving
pickled garlic shoots or capers for
  serving

6 To make the beetroot purée and vinaigrette, place a saucepan over a medium heat, pour in the vinegar and add the beetroot, cloves and sugar. Bring to the boil and simmer until the beetroot is tender and the liquid has reduced. Remove the cloves and strain the liquid into a jug. Purée the beetroot with a little of the reserved juice in a food processor and set aside. Combine the olive oil with the remaining reserved liquid, season with salt and pepper and whisk.

7 Heat an oiled ovenproof frying pan over a high heat and sear the lamb for 3 minutes on each side. Place in the oven for 5–10 minutes or until cooked to your liking. Remove, spoon the pan juices over and rest for 10 minutes. Cut into even slices on an angle.

8 Spoon the beetroot purée and the asparagus purée on to serving plates and arrange the micro-greens, asparagus spears and garlic shoots on top. Scatter the carrot flowers around the salad. Place the mushrooms to one side and top with the lamb. Arrange the potatoes and courgettes on the other side. Drizzle with the beetroot vinaigrette.

Herb-crusted lamb rack with kumara salad and spicy Thai dressing

Recipe by Phillip Maultsaid
Serves 4
Preparation time: 20 minutes
Cooking time: 45 minutes

2 lamb racks
salt and freshly ground black
  pepper
2 slices day-old bread, crusts
  removed
large handful flat-leaf parsley,
  finely chopped
small handful coriander, finely
  chopped
2 sprigs thyme, leaves only, finely
  chopped
1 sprig rosemary, leaves only, finely
  chopped
¼ cup grated Parmesan
1 tsp Dijon mustard
4 golden kumara, peeled
small handful green beans, tops
  and tails removed

Dressing
2 tbsp sesame oil
2 tbsp olive oil
80ml light soy sauce
2 tbsp lemon juice
1 tbsp fish sauce
2 red chilli, de-seeded and finely
  sliced
1 tsp brown sugar
coriander leaves for serving

1 Preheat the oven to 200°C.

2 Score the lamb and rub with salt and pepper. Heat an oiled frying pan over a high heat and sear the lamb for 2–3 minutes on all sides. Place in the oven for 10–15 minutes or until cooked to your liking. Remove from the oven, cover with tinfoil and set aside to rest for 10 minutes.

3 To make the herb crust, put the bread in a food processor and process to make fine breadcrumbs. Place in a bowl with the chopped herbs and Parmesan and combine. Rub the lamb with the mustard and coat in the herbed crumbs. Put the lamb back in the oven for 5 minutes. Remove and slice into cutlets.

4 Place the kumara in a saucepan, cover with salted water and bring to the boil. Reduce the heat and simmer until just tender. Drain and pat dry with paper towels. Cut the kumara into wedges. Heat an oiled frying pan over a medium heat and cook the kumara for 3–5 minutes on each side until golden.

5 Bring a saucepan of salted water to the boil, then reduce to a simmer. Blanch the beans for 2–3 minutes or until tender. Drain.

6 To make the dressing, place the oils, soy sauce, lemon juice, fish sauce, chilli and brown sugar in a bowl and whisk together well. Season with salt and pepper.

7 Pile the kumara wedges and beans in the centre of each place and lean 2 cutlets against the pile. Spoon the dressing over and top with coriander.

This is a dish I came up with after much deliberation, trial and error to cook for the judges at my audition. I wanted to do something that was very Kiwi, and something that could be done comfortably in the time limit, so lamb was an easy choice. I used lots of fresh herbs that work well with lamb for the crust, which looks great on the plate too. I knew that Ray McVinnie liked kumara, which was perfect, as kumara and lamb complement each other beautifully. I used a spicy Thai dressing to add a bit of punch. Ray McVinnie commented, 'It works really well and I would pay good money for that in a restaurant.'

Peppered lamb with asparagus, white bean purée and spring salad

This dish was something I knew I wanted to cook straight away as I really believe in cooking with seasonal, fresh produce and spring is such a great time of year for some of my favourite foods. I've always looked up to and sought advice from my cousin Matt Bouterey, who owns his own restaurant in Richmond, Nelson, so obviously I ran my idea past him — he thought it sounded great. My favourite part of this dish is the combination of the sweet peppery basil and the zesty lemon in the spring salad garnish; it is a delight to the senses when coupled with a tender piece of New Zealand lamb loin.

Recipe by Sarah Irvine
Serves 4
Preparation time: 24 hours (to soak beans) + 15 minutes
Cooking time: 45 minutes

500g haricot beans
1 tbsp salt
4 lamb loins, trimmed
coarsely ground black pepper
grapeseed oil for frying
4 firm vine-ripened tomatoes, halved
1 tbsp chopped thyme leaves
6 cloves garlic, peeled
1 bunch asparagus, stalks peeled
½ cup lemon juice
olive oil
handful Kalamata olives in oil, cut in half lengthwise
small handful flat-leaf parsley
small handful basil leaves

1 Place the beans in a large bowl and cover with cold water. Soak for 24 hours. Once soaked, remove the outer shells and discard. Rinse the beans and drain. Put the beans in a large saucepan, cover with water and boil for 35 minutes. After 20 minutes, add the salt.

2 Preheat the oven to 200°C.

3 Coat the lamb loins well in coarsely ground black pepper. Heat an ovenproof frying pan over a high heat and add grapeseed oil. When hot, sear the lamb all over until slightly browned. Sprinkle the tomatoes with thyme, and add to the pan with garlic cloves. Place lamb in the oven for 8–10 minutes or until cooked to your liking. Remove the lamb, cover with tinfoil and rest for 5 minutes. Slice when ready to serve. Reserve the garlic and tomatoes.

4 Bring a saucepan of salted water to the boil, then reduce to a simmer. Blanch the asparagus for 2–3 minutes. Remove and refresh in a bowl of iced water. Trim the ends.

5 Drain the beans and place in a food processor. Process until coarse, adding the roasted garlic cloves, one at a time, with the motor running. Taste. Add the lemon juice, olive oil and salt and pepper to taste and continue to process until smooth.

6 Combine the olives, parsley and basil in a bowl. Add the roasted tomatoes and drizzle with some oil from the olives. Carefully mix, using your using hands.

7 To serve, spoon the bean purée on to each plate and arrange the asparagus to one side. Place the lamb slices on the other side and scatter with the salad.

Simon's Ragoût

Recipe by Simon Gault
Serves 8–10
Preparation time: 20 minutes
Cooking time: 2 hours

extra-virgin olive oil
½ cup plain flour
salt and freshly ground black
  pepper
1kg lamb leg, trimmed of sinew and
  cut into 2.5cm dice
1kg beef chuck, cut into 2.5cm dice
2 cloves garlic, crushed
2 large onions, finely diced
4 large carrots, peeled and finely
  diced
4 sticks celery, peeled and finely
  diced
2 tbsp tomato paste
1 tbsp smoked paprika
½ tsp black peppercorns, crushed
2 tbsp Lee & Perrins Worcestershire
  Sauce
1 cup red wine
¼ cup Marsala
1 cup vegetable stock
1 tbsp chopped thyme
1 tbsp chopped rosemary
2 bay leaves

1 Heat some olive oil in a saucepan over a medium heat. Place the flour in a bowl and season with salt and pepper. Lightly dust the lamb with the flour. Place in the pan and brown all over, then remove and set aside. Drizzle the pan with more olive oil and place back over a medium heat. Toss the beef in the seasoned flour. Place in the pan and brown all over, then remove from the pan and set aside.

2 Place the saucepan back over a medium heat and drizzle with oil. Sauté the garlic, onions, carrots and celery until soft. Add the tomato paste and smoked paprika, and cook for a further few minutes.

3 Return the meats to the pan and add the crushed peppercorns, Worcestershire Sauce, wine, Marsala, vegetable stock, thyme, rosemary and bay leaves. Season with salt and pepper. Cover and simmer over a low heat for 1½ – 2 hours or until the lamb and beef are tender.

4 Serve with beans and potato gnocchi or mashed potato.

Roast stuffed lamb fillet wrapped in prosciutto with kumara chip and carrot purée stack, minted pea foam and mint oil

On the show, I wasn't 100 per cent happy with this dish and would have liked a bit more time to perfect the processes involved. It was a bit of an invention test for me, as my experience with lamb was limited. But it all worked out in the end. Kiwi culture and lamb go hand in hand, so here's a bit of elegant Kiwiana for ya!

Recipe by Kelly Young
Serves 2
Preparation time: 20 minutes
Cooking time: 1 hour

2 tbsp finely chopped mint leaves
2 tbsp finely chopped rosemary
¼ cup pine nuts, toasted
¼ cup finely grated Parmesan
olive oil for drizzling
salt and freshly ground black
 pepper
8 slices prosciutto di Parma
2 180g lamb backstraps
extra-virgin olive oil for drizzling

Carrot purée
2 shallots, finely diced
30g butter
1 cup vegetable stock
2 small carrots, peeled and diced
1 tsp honey
¼ cup cream

Kumara chips
canola oil for deep-frying
2 kumara, peeled and thinly sliced
2 cloves garlic, halved

1 Preheat the oven to 200°C.

2 Place the mint, rosemary, pine nuts and Parmesan in a blender, pour in a drizzle of olive oil and blend to a paste.

3 Place the prosciutto slices, slightly overlapping, on a flat surface. Cut the lamb backstraps in half lengthwise and flatten, only cutting two-thirds of the way through the meat. Drizzle the lamb halves with extra-virgin olive oil and season with salt and pepper. Spread the herb paste across the fillets and fold each over to enclose the paste. Place on the prosciutto slices and roll up tightly. Set aside.

4 To make the carrot purée, heat a frying pan over a medium heat. Sauté the shallots in the butter until soft. Add the vegetable stock, carrots and honey and cook 10–12 minutes, slightly reducing the liquid. Pour the cream in another saucepan and place over a low heat to warm, then add to the carrots and season to taste. Strain off the liquid and reserve. Using a stick blender, blend into a purée, using as much of the liquid as required to purée without beccoming runny.

5 Half fill a saucepan with canola oil and heat to 180°C to deep-fry the kumara.

6 Rub the kumara discs with garlic, then deep-fry in batches until golden and crisp. Drain on paper towels and season with salt.

7 To make the mint oil, place the mint, caster sugar and oil in a blender and blend until combined. Set aside in the fridge.

8 To make the minted pea foam, bring the cream and vegetable stock to the boil, then add the peas and cook for 3 minutes. Add the mint and cook

(continued overleaf)

Mint oil
½ cup mint leaves
¼ tsp caster sugar
100ml olive oil

Minted pea foam
1 cup cream
¼ cup vegetable stock
½ cup peas
¼ cup of mint
salt and freshly ground black
  pepper

for 1 minute, then transfer to a blender and blend until smooth. Strain the mixture into a clean bowl. Just before serving, season and blend with a stick blender to make a foam.

9 To cook the lamb, heat an oiled ovenproof frying pan over a medium heat. Sear the lamb rolls for 2–3 minutes on each side, turning to brown all over. Place the pan in the oven for 8–10 minutes or until the lamb is cooked to your liking. Remove and rest for 6–8 minutes. Cut into slices on an angle.

10 To serve, place a kumara chip on a plate and top with a spoonful of carrot purée. Repeat and finish with a kumara chip. Repeat for the other serving. Arrange the lamb slices to one side and drizzle with mint oil. Spoon the minted pea foam around the kumara and carrot stack.

Duo of lamb racks with mash, pea purée, baby carrots and red wine reduction

This was one of my favourite dishes to create. We were told about a New Zealand challenge using lamb. I wanted to create a dish that any Kiwi could recreate at home using ingredients that most would already have in the fridge. It turned out to be a very significant dish for me — the judges loved it and summed it up as a good old 'meat and three veg' type of meal. I must admit, the crust on the lamb is delicious and a good trick to enhance the flavour is to make a hole through the centre of the rack and squeeze the butter through it. For the pea purée it is a good idea to boil the peas in good chicken stock for a short time, then pass the peas through a sieve to get a bright tasty purée. What an absolute taste sensation.

Recipe by Brett McGregor
Serves 2
Preparation time: 30 minutes
Cooking time: 1 hour

2 lamb racks
olive oil for drizzling
salt and fresly ground black pepper

Herb crust
1 clove garlic, crushed
1 tbsp finely chopped thyme leaves
1 tbsp finely chopped flat-leaf parsley
1 tbsp finely chopped mint
2 tbsp pine nuts, finely chopped
zest of ½ lemon
1 tbsp Dijon mustard

Herb butter
30g butter
1 tbsp finely chopped flat-leaf parsley
1 tbsp finely chopped thyme leaves
1 tbsp finely chopped mint leaves

Mash
2 potatoes, peeled and diced
1 kumara, peeled and diced
2 cloves garlic, crushed
100ml cream
30g butter

1 Preheat the oven to 200°C.

2 Trim the lamb racks, de-bone one rack and scrape the bones clean on the other. Drizzle with the olive oil, and season with salt and pepper.

3 Combine the garlic, thyme, parsley, mint, pine nuts and lemon zest in a bowl. Spread the mustard over the meat of the de-boned rack, then coat in the herb mixture.

4 To make the herb butter, combine the butter, parsley, thyme and mint in a bowl. Using a knife, create a pocket between the meat and bone of the other rack, and stuff with the herb butter.

5 Heat an oiled frying pan over a medium heat and sear the lamb racks for 3–6 minutes on all sides until browned. Place both racks on an oven tray and put in the oven for 8–15 minutes or until cooked to your liking. Rest for 10 minutes. Slice the crusted rack into thick slices, and slice the end off the stuffed rack.

6 To make the mash, place the potatoes, kumara and garlic in a saucepan, cover with water and lightly salt. Place over a high heat, bring to the boil, then reduce to a simmer and cook for 8–12 minutes or until tender. Drain well. Mash the vegetables through a sieve into a clean saucepan, then add the cream and butter, and season with salt and pepper. Whip until creamy.

7 To make the pea purée, heat a frying pan over a medium heat. Add the shallots and butter and sauté until soft. Pour the stock and water into a saucepan and place over a medium heat. Bring to the boil, add the peas and cook for 3–4 minutes or until the peas are soft but still green. Add the

(continued overleaf)

Pea purée

2 shallots, finely diced
50g butter
100ml vegetable stock
100ml water
1 cup frozen peas
small handful mint leaves

Baby carrots

8 baby carrots, cleaned
30g butter
1 tbsp honey

Red wine reduction

2 shallots, sliced
1 clove garlic, sliced
200ml red wine
1 tbsp balsamic vinegar
1 sprig rosemary
1 bay leaf
80g butter, diced

mint leaves and cook for 1 minute. Drain and reserve the cooking liquid. Place the shallots, peas and mint into a blender and blend to a purée, adding enough of the reserved liquid to make a smooth purée. Season with salt and pepper, and add a drizzle of olive oil.

8 Bring a saucepan of salted water to the boil, then reduce to a simmer. Add the carrots and cook for 4–8 minutes or until just tender. Drain and return the carrots to the saucepan with the butter and honey. Cook until lightly caramelised, and season with salt and pepper.

9 To make the red wine reduction, heat an oiled frying pan over a medium heat. Sauté the shallots and garlic for 1–2 minutes until soft. Add the red wine, vinegar, rosemary and bay leaf, and simmer to reduce the liquid by three-quarters. Season with salt and pepper. Remove from the heat and strain through a sieve into a clean saucepan. Whisk in the butter, a small amount at a time, to make a thick, glossy sauce.

10 To serve, smear the pea purée over a plate and top with the crusted lamb rack. Place the stuffed lamb and a quenelle of mash alongside. Arrange the baby carrots on the mash and spoon the red wine reduction onto the plate.

Beef carpaccio with summer salad, parsnip chips and Bloody Mary shots

I really loved this dish. It met all of my criteria and illustrated my philosophy on food — that it should offer contrast, be enjoyed with a good drink, and should always be an adventure of experimentation and development. The highlight of my MasterChef experience was during the judging of this dish. Simon commented that my Bloody Mary was 'bloody marvellous'. He and Ross also gave me a couple of tips for variations on the Bloody Mary, including adding a dash of sherry. Ross was also really positive about my dish, saying that he would happily pay for it. This dish is something I continue to make for friends and family as an entrée, or simply as a grazing dish for a lazy Sunday lunch. It always goes down well with a carafe of Bloody Mary or a gorgeous bottle of red wine and some fresh crusty French bread.

Recipe by Fiona McDonald
Serves 4
Preparation time: 1½ hours to
  freeze carpaccio + 30 minutes
Cooking time: 20 minutes

300g beef fillet, trimmed
4 tbsp Dijon mustard
freshly ground black pepper

Parsnip chips
vegetable oil for deep-frying
2 parsnips, peeled and shaved

Summer salad
2 tbsp balsamic vinegar
6 tbsp olive oil
juice of 1 lemon
1 tsp wholegrain mustard
salt and freshly ground black pepper
2 avocados, finely diced
big handful micro-greens
2 grapefruit, peeled and segmented

1 Spread the mustard over the beef, then roll in enough ground black pepper to form a crust. Heat an oiled frying pan over a high heat and sear the beef for 1 minute on each side, just enough to harden the crust. Cool, then wrap very tightly in clingfilm and place in the freezer for 1½ hours until the beef just begins to freeze. This gives the beef a neat, round shape.

2 Fill a saucepan one-third full of vegetable oil and heat to 180°C to deep-fry the parsnip chips. Fry the parsnip chips in batches until golden brown, being careful not to burn them. Drain on paper towels and season with salt and pepper.

3 To make the salad dressing, combine the vinegar, olive oil, lemon juice and wholegrain mustard in a bowl. Mix well and season with salt and pepper. Place a ring mould in the centre of a serving plate. Put the diced avocado in the bottom of the mould and drizzle with some dressing. Top with micro-greens and another light drizzle of the dressing. Arrange the grapefruit segments on top in a flower shape and lightly dress again. Repeat for other serving.

4 To make the Bloody Mary shots, mix the tomato juice, vodka and Worcestershire Sauce in a jug and chill. Pour into shot glasses and finish with freshly ground black pepper and a celery stick just before serving.

5 To make the dressing, combine the crème fraîche, lemon juice and mustard in a bowl, and season with salt and pepper. Remove the beef from the freezer and unwrap half of the beef. Using a very sharp knife, slice the beef as finely as possible, being careful not to tear the beef. Unwrap the remaining half and slice. Lay out a sheet of clingfilm on a flat surface,

(continued overleaf)

Bloody Mary shots

2 cups spicy tomato juice
½ cup vodka
Lee & Perrins Worcestershire Sauce
  to taste
celery sticks for serving

Crème fraîche dressing

4 tbsp crème fraîche
juice of 1 lemon
½ tsp Dijon mustard

lightly oil and place the beef slices across it. Place another oiled sheet of clingfilm on top and gently roll the beef with a rolling pin to make it thinner.

6 To serve, place the beef slices around the salad mould, squeeze lemon juice over the meat and drizzle with the crème fraîche dressing. Remove the salad mould and top the salad with parsnip crisps. Serve with Bloody Mary shots.

Port peppered eye fillet with creamy mushroom and wholegrain mustard sauce, and parsnip and carrot minted mash

This was my audition dish. I knew that on the day my nerves would be close to uncontrollable and the pressure would be tough so I wanted to keep it simple yet tasty. The key to this dish is to source a great local butcher and a fresh produce market to get the freshest, tastiest ingredients.

Recipe by Kelly Young
Serves 2
Preparation time: 30 minutes
Cooking time: 45 minutes

2 200g beef eye fillets
1 tsp red and black pepper
  seasoning
¼ cup port

Mash
2 parsnips, peeled and chopped
2 carrots, peeled and chopped
20g butter
1 tbsp finely chopped fresh mint

Mushroom and mustard sauce
1 onion, finely diced
20g butter
80g button mushrooms, finely
  sliced
100ml cream
1 tbsp wholegrain mustard

½ bunch asparagus
sprig of mint for serving

1 Place the eye fillets in a bowl, sprinkle with the pepper seasoning and pour the port over. Set aside to marinate for 30 minutes.

2 Preheat the oven to 180°C.

3 To make the mash, bring a saucepan of salted water to the boil. Add the parsnips and carrots and cook for 10–12 minutes until tender. Drain well, then add the butter and mash until smooth. Season with salt and pepper, and stir through the chopped mint. Set aside.

4 Heat an oiled ovenproof frying pan over a high heat and sear the fillets for 2 minutes on each side. Place the pan in the oven for 6–8 minutes or until the beef is cooked to your liking. Remove and rest for 5 minutes. Cut into thick slices.

5 To make the mustard sauce, heat a frying pan over a medium heat and sauté the onion in the butter for 3–4 minutes or until soft. Add the mushrooms and continue to cook until soft. Add the cream and the mustard, lower the heat and simmer, stirring occasionally. Reduce until the sauce coats the back of a spoon.

6 Bring a saucepan of water to the boil, then reduce to a simmer. Place the asparagus in a steamer and put over the simmering water. Cover and steam for 3–4 minutes or until the asparagus is tender.

7 To serve, spoon the mash and mustard sauce next to each other onto each plate. Place slices of beef down the middle of the mash and sauce, and the asparagus to the side. Finish with a sprig of mint.

Fillet of beef with a creamy mustard mash and red wine jus

This was my audition dish that kicked off the whole MasterChef culinary journey for me. I have made this meal, and variations of it, so many times for family and friends. I've also made it with a lovely backstrap of wild venison — amazing! Good-quality meat is essential, of course, but what really sold it to the judges was the potato mash. Simon loved it! I've modified my recipe over the years, and now use a small amount of butter and olive oil, as well as a little milk, a sprinkling of fresh Parmesan and wholegrain mustard, which just kicks it up a notch — and matches perfectly with the beef, of course.

Tip: Throw in a couple of cloves of garlic when you are boiling your potatoes, then mash them in — they give a lovely fragrance and a subtle hint of garlic. Drain your boiled potatoes, then put them back on the stovetop for 30 seconds or so to get rid of all the water, which makes for a better mash. Use a potato ricer or mouli, or push the boiled potato through a sieve to get rid of all lumps.

Recipe by Steve Juergens
Serves 4
Preparation time: 4 hours for jus
  + 15 minutes
Cooking time: 45 minutes

Red wine jus
1kg beef bones
1 onion, diced
2 carrots, peeled and chopped
2 sticks celery, chopped
2 leeks (white part only), chopped
1 bottle Shiraz
3 star anise
1 tsp sugar

Creamy mash
4 potatoes, peeled and cut into
  1cm-thick slices
3 cloves garlic, peeled
150g butter
olive oil for drizzling
salt and freshly ground black
  pepper
2 tbsp milk
1 tsp wholegrain mustard
3 tbsp grated Parmesan

1 To make the jus, heat a large oiled saucepan over a high heat. Add the beef bones and brown all over, then add the onion, carrots, celery and leeks and continue to brown. Cover with cold water and bring to the boil. Reduce the heat and simmer for 3–4 hours, skimming off the fat every half-hour. Line a sieve with muslin and strain the stock into a clean saucepan. Bring the stock back to a simmer and continue to reduce. Pour the Shiraz into another saucepan with the star anise and sugar, and place over a medium heat. Simmer and reduce by half. Add the reduced wine to the stock and simmer for a further 20 minutes. Set aside.

2 To make the mash, bring a saucepan of salted water to the boil. Add the potatoes and garlic and cook until tender. Drain, then place back over a low heat to steam off the excess moisture. Mash the potato and garlic through a sieve, then add the butter, drizzle with olive oil and season with salt and pepper. Add the milk, mustard and Parmesan and mix well. Cover with tinfoil and set aside.

3 Preheat the oven to 210°C.

4 Season the eye fillet well all over with the pepper and salt. Heat an oiled ovenproof frying pan over a high heat and sear the beef for 4 minutes until browned on all sides. Place in the oven for 7 minutes or until cooked to your liking. Take out of the oven and rest for 10 minutes. Cut into 6cm thick slices.

5 Place the mushrooms and tomatoes in a roasting tray, drizzle with olive oil and season with salt and pepper. Place in the oven for 10–15 minutes.

(continued overleaf)

1 x 800g piece eye fillet, trimmed
black pepper
Maldon sea salt
4 field mushrooms
8 vine-ripened tomatoes
2 bunches English spinach, stems
  trimmed

6 Bring a saucepan of salted water to the boil and blanch the spinach for a
few seconds. Drain well.

7 To serve, place a ring mould in the centre of each plate and spoon
the mash into the ring. Top with blanched spinach, then a mushroom.
Carefully remove the ring. Place the beef on top of the mushroom. Spoon
a small amount of jus over the beef and around the plates. Place the
tomatoes to the side and pour the remaining jus into a serving jug.

Peppered eye fillet with green beans, hand-cut fries and Béarnaise sauce

Ellerslie Race Day
Serves 4
Preparation time: 20 minutes
Cooking time: 50 minutes

Fries
canola oil for deep-frying
4 Agria potatoes, peeled and cut
    into 2cm-thick chips
salt

Eye fillet
½ cup whole peppercorns
1 small whole beef fillet, silver skin
    removed
salt to taste

Béarnaise sauce
225g unsalted butter
2 shallots, finely diced
3 tbsp finely chopped fresh
    tarragon
¼ cup white wine vinegar
pinch of white pepper
2 tbsp water
3 egg yolks
lemon juice to taste

1 handful green beans, trimmed
1 clove garlic, finely chopped

1 Preheat the oven to 220°C.

2 Heat canola oil in a deep fryer to 180°C.

3 Par-cook the chips in batches and drain on paper towels. When ready to serve, deep-fry until golden and crisp. Season with salt.

4 Pound the peppercorns in a mortar and pestle until well cracked. Coat the beef with the cracked pepper and season with salt. Heat a chargrill pan over a high heat until hot. Sear the fillet, turning to get dark char marks on all sides, for 2–3 minutes in total. Transfer to a roasting dish and place in the oven for 12–16 minutes for medium-rare or until cooked to your liking. Remove from the oven and rest for 10 minutes. Slice into 8 pieces.

5 To make the Béarnaise, first clarify the butter by gently melting it in a saucepan over a low heat. Remove from the heat and carefully pour the golden clear liquid into a jug, leaving behind the milky solids. Cool a little.

6 Combine the shallots, 2 tablespoons of the tarragon, vinegar, pepper and water in a small saucepan, place over a low-medium heat and simmer to reduce to 1 tablespoon of liquid. Strain the liquid through a fine sieve. Bring a saucepan of water to the boil, then reduce to a simmer. Pour the reduced liquid into a bowl that sits on the saucepan above the simmering water. Add the egg yolks and whisk continuously over a medium heat until thick and foamy, being careful not to scramble the eggs. Whisk in the butter, a little at a time, over the heat. When all the butter is incorporated the sauce should be thick and creamy. Stir through lemon juice to taste and the remaining tarragon.

7 To cook the beans, bring a saucepan of salted water to the boil, then reduce to a simmer. Blanch the beans until tender, then drain and refresh in ice-cold water. Heat an oiled frying pan over a medium heat and sauté the garlic and beans. Season.

The secret to cooking any piece of meat is to give it time to rest. This redistributes the juices throughout the meat, making it juicy and succulent. The other key part to this recipe is the Béarnaise sauce. It can be a bit tricky, but just make sure you don't over-cook the egg yolks at the start, and add the butter very slowly so the sauce doesn't split.
Tracey Gunn, Ellerslie Challenge

Beef, bacon and Guinness hot pot pie

Recipe by Nigel Anderson
Serves 4
Preparation time: 30 minutes
Cooking time: 2½ hours

shortcrust pastry (see recipe on
  page 44)
flour for dusting
salt and freshly ground black
  pepper
700g beef rump, diced
200g rindless bacon, diced
1 onion, finely diced
2 cloves garlic, crushed
1 cup finely sliced button
  mushrooms
30g butter
2 tbsp tomato paste
1 can Guinness
750ml beef stock
3 tbsp finely chopped fresh thyme
  leaves
4 medium potatoes, thinly sliced

1 Prepare the pastry, following the recipe on page 44.

2 Heat an oiled frying pan over a medium-high heat. Combine some flour, salt and pepper in a bowl and toss the beef through until lightly coated. Place the beef in the pan and cook until browned all over. Remove from the pan.

3 Place the pan back over a medium heat, and sauté the bacon, onion, garlic and mushrooms in the butter until soft. Return the browned beef to the pan with the tomato paste, Guinness and stock. Reduce the heat and simmer for 2 hours or until the sauce has reduced and thickened. Season to taste and stir in the thyme.

4 Preheat the oven to 180°C.

5 Bring a saucepan of salted water to the boil, then reduce to a simmer. Parboil the sliced potato for 3–4 minutes, then drain and pat dry.

6 Spoon the filling into the prepared pastry shell, top with the potato slices, brush with oil and add salt and pepper to season. Bake in the oven for 45 minutes or until the potato is golden.

My wife, Charlie, does a very similar dish at home, which is a huge favourite with the whole family. As soon as I saw the Guinness in the pantry, that was it. The key to this dish is to cook the filling as long and slowly as possible — ideally, for 2–3 hours. This will allow the sauce to reduce to almost nothing. You will be rewarded with beautifully tender meat and an intensely flavoured sauce. Any topping can be used — pastry, mashed potato or the finely sliced potatoes I have used here.

Szechuan beef stir-fry

Recipe by Steve Juergens
Serves 2
Preparation time: 20 minutes
Cooking time: 10 minutes

200g beef fillet, cut into strips
1 tbsp soy sauce
oil for frying
1 medium onion, finely chopped
1 tsp finely chopped garlic
1 tsp finely chopped ginger
½ red chilli, de-seeded and finely
  chopped
50g mushrooms, finely sliced
50g medium carrots, julienned
50g red capsicum, julienned
½ tsp salt
2 tbsp Szechuan pepper
12 snow peas, sliced in half
  diagonally
1 tbsp oyster sauce
2 tbsp hoisin sauce
¼ cup beef stock
250g egg noodles
50g spring onions, sliced
50g bean sprouts
fresh coriander leaves to garnish

1 Place the beef strips in soy sauce.
Set aside.

2 Heat a wok to high, add some oil
and stir-fry the onion, garlic, ginger and chilli for 2–3 minutes. Set aside.

3 Stir-fry the mushrooms, carrots and capsicum for 2–3 minutes and
set aside.

4 Grind the salt and Szechuan pepper together in a mortar and pestle.
Remove the beef from the soy sauce and coat with the salt and pepper
mixture, add to the hot wok and stir-fry for 2 minutes. Then add the snow
peas, the oyster and hoisin sauces and beef stock, and cook for a few
minutes. Add the onion and vegetable mixtures back into the wok with the
noodles and spring onions, and cook for a further minute.

5 Serve in a large bowl, garnished with bean sprouts and coriander leaves.

*Stir-fries really are so simple — you throw everything in a wok, cook
and it's done. You can use beef, chicken, pork, seafood, or make it
vegetarian — whatever you enjoy or feel like. I love cooking stir-fries
because they are quick and nutritious — easy to do after a long day
and usually faster than getting takeaways. Always cook the meat
separately, then set it aside and cook the vegetables. Everything then
goes back in the wok to combine and it's done. You can serve the stir-
fry on its own, or add noodles or rice. A little sprinkling of sesame
seeds over the stir-fry right before you serve looks and tastes great.
Have fun — experiment!*

Beef with hoisin sauce and vegetables, chilli and sesame seeds

Recipe by Sue Drummond
Serves 4
Preparation time: 20 minutes
Cooking time: 10 minutes

2 onion
6 cloves garlic, finely chopped
1 red chilli, de-seeded and finely
    sliced (reserve some for garnish)
2 tbsp hoisin sauce
2 tbsp kecap manis
2 tsp chilli oil, plus extra for frying
20cm piece beef eye fillet, cut into
    thin strips
1 carrot, peeled and julienned
1 red capsicum, cored and julienned
3 small bunches bok choy, cut and
    trimmed
4 tbsp soy sauce
4 tbsp cornflour
2 tbsp sesame seeds, lightly toasted
4 spring onions (white part only),
    cut into 3cm pieces

1 To make the marinade, finely chop half the onion and combine in a bowl with the garlic, chilli, hoisin sauce, kecap manis and chilli oil. Add the beef strips, mix to coat and marinate for 1 hour.

2 Heat a wok to high and add some chilli oil. Cut the remaining onion into 2cm squares and add with the carrot, capsicum and bok choy. Stir-fry lightly for 2 minutes. Remove and set aside.

3 Stir-fry the beef for 2–3 minutes.

4 Return the vegetables to the wok and add a little more hoisin sauce, ¼ cup water, the soy sauce and cornflour. Stir-fry for a few minutes.

5 Serve in a bowl and top with the extra chilli, toasted sesame seeds and spring onion.

I invented this recipe for the Chinese challenge. We often eat dishes like this at home — I love to combine meat and fresh vegetables to create a fresh and satisfying meal. I love Chinese food as I find it enables you to produce quick and wholesome meals. Over the years I seem to cook more of the Asian style of cooking. You usually feel rather good after a meal of Chinese food, especially if no MSG is added.

Crab and lime salad and Thai beef salad

Recipe by Brett McGregor
Serves 2
Preparation time: 30 minutes
Cooking time: 45 minutes

Crab and lime salad

300g Alaskan crab meat
½ cucumber
1 red chilli, de-seeded and finely chopped
2 shallots, finely sliced
small handful coriander leaves
grated zest of 1 lime
2 tbsp mint leaves
lime wedges for serving

Crab salad dressing

3 tbsp lime juice
2 tbsp coconut vinegar
1 tsp sesame oil
1 tbsp olive oil
2 tsp fish sauce

Thai beef salad

200g beef fillet
olive oil for rubbing
salt and freshly ground black pepper
2 shallots, diced
small handful mint leaves
small handful coriander leaves
1 red capsicum, cored and finely sliced
1 red chilli, de-seeded and finely sliced
1 spring onion, sliced on an angle

Beef salad dressing

grated zest of 1 lime
¼ cup lime juice
2 cloves garlic, crushed
3 tbsp fish sauce
2 tsp palm sugar

1 To make the crab and lime salad, shred the crab meat into a bowl.

2 Slice the cucumber in half lengthwise, scoop out the seeds and finely slice on an angle. Combine the chilli, shallots, coriander, lime zest, cucumber and mint leaves in a bowl, then mix in the crab meat.

3 To make the crab and lime salad dressing, place all the ingredients in a bowl and whisk to combine. Dress the salad just before serving.

4 To make the Thai beef salad, rub the beef fillet with olive oil and season with salt and pepper. Heat a frying pan over a high heat and sear the beef on all sides then place in the oven (pre-heated to 180ºC) for 5 minutes. Set aside to cool, then put in the fridge.

5 Place the shallots in a bowl of iced water to allow them to crisp.

6 Combine the mint, coriander, capsicum and chilli in a bowl. Finely slice the beef and drain the shallots. Carefully fold the beef, shallots and spring onion into the salad.

7 To make the beef salad dressing, place all the ingredients in a bowl, season with black pepper and whisk to combine. Dress the salad just before serving.

8 Spoon the crab and lime salad on one side of a large serving platter and garnish with lime wedges. Spoon the Thai beef salad on the other side. Serve immediately.

This is something my wife, Tracey, helped with, without even knowing it. She has always created a beautiful Thai beef salad we eat religiously at home throughout summer. I wanted to create something that I have not seen before and came up with this idea for a dish that uses some Alaskan king crab with a beautiful cut of beef fillet. These two very different dishes complement each other nicely. This is a great dish to eat at any time, but the Thai influences create something quite delicate yet tasty. You may have some trouble locating the coconut vinegar but it really adds a new dimension to this dish. Superb.

Antoine's red Thai curry tripe

Recipe by Tony Astle
Serves 2
Preparation time: overnight for
    tripe + 4 hours
Cooking time: 1 hour

Tripe

1 whole bleached (1kg) export-
    quality honeycomb sheep tripe
1 bouquet garni (thyme, bay leaf
    and parsley stalks)

Red curry paste

7 dried red chillies
½ tsp white peppercorns
1 tsp coriander seeds
½ tsp cumin seeds
1 tsp shrimp paste
2 shallots, finely chopped
5 cloves garlic, finely chopped
1 stalk lemongrass (white part
    only), finely diced
1 tsp finely diced ginger
3 coriander roots, finely sliced
1 kaffir lime leaf, finely chopped

Thai curry sauce

1 tbsp finely diced garlic
1 tbsp finely diced ginger
3½ tbsp red curry paste
2½ tbsp tomato paste
10g palm sugar
250ml chicken stock
500ml coconut cream
1 large onion, very finely diced
3 cloves garlic, finely diced
100g rindless bacon, finely chopped
¼ cup coriander leaves, chopped
    roughly, plus extra for serving
3 spring onions (white part only),
    finely sliced on three-quarter angle
juice of 2 limes
fish sauce to taste
8 quail eggs, soft-boiled for serving
bean shoots for serving
½ telegraph cucumber, julienned

1 To cook the tripe, place in a large saucepan with the bouquet garni and cover with cold water. Bring to the boil, reduce the heat and simmer for 3–4 hours or until tender — the longer you boil it, the more tender it will become. Do not salt the water or the tripe will become too salty. Keep water topped up if it runs too low.

2 Remove the tripe from the saucepan and strain, reserving the stock. Refrigerate overnight to allow the stock to set. It will form a jelly.

3 Preheat the oven to 180°C.

4 To make the curry paste, place the chillies in a bowl and cover with boiling water. Set aside to soak for 10 minutes, then drain, de-seed and roughly chop. Wrap the peppercorns, coriander seeds, cumin seeds and shrimp paste in foil and bake for 8–12 minutes or until fragrant. Place the chillies and spice mixture with the remaining paste ingredients in a mortar and pestle and pound to a smooth paste.

5 To make the sauce, heat an oiled frying pan to medium and sauté the garlic and ginger for 3 minutes. Add the curry paste, tomato paste and palm sugar, and sauté for another 2–3 minutes. Stir in the chicken stock and coconut cream and turn up the heat. Allow the sauce to reduce by around one-third until it is a sauce consistency. Set aside until needed.

6 To cook the tripe, heat an oiled frying pan over a medium heat. Cook the onion, garlic and bacon until soft. Cut the tripe into 2cm cubes and add to the pan with the tripe juices, and allow to simmer until most of the liquid has evaporated. Add the Thai curry sauce and bring to the boil, then reduce the heat and simmer until heated through.

7 Stir in the chopped coriander and spring onions, and season to taste with the lime juice and fish sauce.

8 To soft-boil the eggs, bring a saucepan of water to the boil, then reduce to a simmer. Boil the eggs for 2 minutes, remove and place in a bowl of iced water to stop cooking. Peel.

9 Spoon the curried tripe into a bowl and arrange the halved quail eggs on top. Finish with bean shoots, cucumber and coriander.

Volcanic pork

This creation is a flamboyant dish full of colour and flavour that reflects my personality. The main trick for this dish is that the pork loin should be marinated overnight in fresh orange juice. The acidity of the juice actually begins to cook the pork. The Coca Cola is used to create a unique caramelised glaze and, when it is mixed with the orange juice, flavours combine into a whole new taste sensation. The great thing about this dish is its ability to create a talking point. After it aired on TV, the dish was spoken about on morning television and people in the streets stopped me to chat about the crazy ingredient choices that I made! It was pretty cool to be noticed for something I had created.

Recipe by Carlos Garcia
Serves 4
Preparation time: overnight to soak
  beans + 20 minutes
Cooking time: 2¾ hours

2 cups fresh orange juice
1 tsp cumin
1 tsp oregano
2 cloves garlic, crushed
salt and freshly ground black
  pepper
olive oil for drizzling
2 medium pork fillets
2 cups Coca Cola

Black bean cake (makes 4 cakes)
100g dried black beans or turtle
  beans
pinch of salt
½ onion, finely chopped
½ red capsicum, cored and finely
  diced
1 tomato, finely diced
2 cloves garlic, finely sliced
2 tbsp chopped fresh coriander
½ cup polenta
100g feta, roughly chopped

Chunky salsa
2 tomatoes, finely diced
1 small red onion, finely diced

1 To make the marinade, combine the orange juice, cumin, oregano and garlic in a bowl, then season with salt and pepper and drizzle with olive oil. Place the pork fillets in the bowl and coat. Transfer the pork and marinade to a plastic bag and refrigerate overnight. Remove from the fridge 1 hour before cooking.

2 To prepare the black beans, place in a bowl and cover with hot water. Cover the bowl and let the beans soak overnight, then drain. Pour 2 litres of water into a saucepan, add the beans and a pinch of salt and bring to the boil. Reduce to a simmer and simmer for 2 hours or until the beans are soft and the liquid has reduced to ½ litre.

3 To make the bean cakes, heat an oiled frying pan over a medium heat, add the onion, capsicum, tomato, garlic and coriander, and cook for 5 minutes. Add the beans and cook for a further few minutes. Cool, then mash.

4 Meanwhile, pour 500ml of water into a saucepan, place over a high heat and bring to the boil. Slowly pour in the polenta and stir continuously until thickened. Combine with the beans and mix well. Spread the mixture over a flat oven tray to a 2cm thickness and refrigerate for 20 minutes to set. Using a biscuit cutter, cut into 7cm rounds.

5 Heat a frying pan over a high heat and sear the pork fillets on all sides, then lower the heat and slowly add the cola. Cover and cook for 8–10 minutes, turning the pork after 5 minutes. Remove the pork, reserving the sauce, and rest for 5 minutes before slicing.

6 Heat an oiled frying pan over a medium heat and lightly fry the black bean cakes on both sides every 3 minutes. Top with the feta.

7 To make the salsa, combine the tomatoes, onion, capsicum and jalapeños in a bowl, then add the coriander and lime juice. Mix well and season with salt.

(continued overleaf)

½ green capsicum, cored and finely
  diced
2 tbsp chopped red jalapeños
½ cup coriander, chopped roughly
juice of 2 limes

Guacamole
1 avocado
juice of 1 lime

8 To make the guacamole, mash the avocado with the lime juice to a chunky consistency. Season with salt and pepper.

9 To serve, place a black-bean cake in the centre of each plate and top with slices of pork to create a 'volcano' shape. Spoon the salsa around the cake and drizzle with the reserved pork sauce. Top with a quenelle of guacamole.

Minestrone

Recipe by MasterChef kitchen
Serves 6–8
Preparation time: 20 minutes
Cooking time: 1½ hours

¼ cup olive oil
100g pancetta, diced
3 cloves garlic, crushed
2 onions, finely diced
2 carrots, peeled and diced
3 courgettes, diced
4 sticks celery, diced
2 potatoes, peeled and diced
2 tbsp tomato paste
1 cup white wine
2 cups chicken stock
1 x 400g tin tomatoes
2 sprigs oregano
2 sprigs thyme
1 bay leaf
1 375g tin cannellini beans, drained
  and rinsed
1 375g tin borlotti beans, drained
  and rinsed
½ cup orzo pasta
8 green beans, trimmed and sliced
handful flat-leaf parsley, roughly
  chopped
salt and freshly ground black
  pepper
extra-virgin olive oil for serving
grated Parmesan for serving

1 Heat a large saucepan over a medium heat, add half the olive oil and sauté the pancetta, garlic and onion for a few minutes. Add the remaining olive oil, carrots, courgettes, celery and potatoes, and cook for 4–8 minutes, stirring occasionally, until the vegetables are soft but not coloured.

2 Add the tomato paste and white wine, and cook for 1 minute. Pour in the stock and tomatoes. Tie the oregano, thyme and bay leaf together with kitchen string and add to the pan. Cover and simmer for 35 minutes, stirring occasionally.

3 Add the cannellini and borlotti beans and the pasta, and cook for a further 10–15 minutes. Then add the green beans in the last 10 minutes of cooking.

4 Season with salt and pepper just before serving. Drizzle with extra-virgin olive oil and finish with freshly grated Parmesan and parsley.

Note: Add extra stock if you prefer a thinner minestrone.

Prosciutto-wrapped chicken and pork with honey-mustard vinaigrette, baby carrots and asparagus

My fiancé, Jamie, loves this dish. Three types of meat and mash — dinner heaven! I was so glad when this dish won over the judges at the audition, especially after having such a difficult time. My meat wasn't cooked properly and I had to think on my feet about how to remedy this, with all three judges standing there watching me — but I managed to plate up in the last 30 seconds. Ray was impressed. Now, if I'm struggling to get dinner on the table, I remember his words of encouragement.

Recipe by Karyn Fisk
Serves 4
Preparation time: 1 hour to
  refrigerate chicken + 20 minutes
Cooking time: 45 minutes

2 tbsp finely chopped oregano leaves
2 tbsp finely chopped rosemary
  leaves
salt
olive oil for rubbing
4 small pork tenderloin
12 slices prosciutto di Parma
4 small chicken breasts

Kumara and potato mash
2 golden kumara, peeled and diced
2 potatoes, peeled and diced
40g butter
½ cup cream
salt and freshly ground black pepper

Honey-mustard vinaigrette
juice of 1 lemon
2 tsp honey
1 tsp English mustard
½ cup white wine vinegar
olive oil
12 baby carrots, cleaned
12 asparagus, trimmed
1 tbsp pine nuts, toasted

1 Crush the oregano and rosemary leaves with the salt in a mortar and pestle. Rub olive oil all over the pork, then coat in the herbs.

2 Place a sheet of clingfilm on a flat surface and place the prosciutto slices on top, slightly overlapping. Butterfly the chicken breasts and place each on top of 3 prosciutto slices. Then place the pork on top of each chicken breast and, using the clingfilm, tightly roll and wrap the entire parcel. Twist the ends of the clingfilm to hold firmly in place. Put in the fridge for 1 hour.

3 To make the mash, place the kumara and potatoes in a saucepan with lightly salted water. Place over a high heat and bring to the boil. Reduce to a simmer and cook until tender. Drain well. Add the butter and cream, and mash until smooth. Season with salt and pepper.

4 Preheat the oven to 180°C.

5 Heat an oiled ovenproof frying pan to high and sear the meat roll on all sides until brown. Place in the oven for 12–15 minutes or until cooked as you like. Rest for 10 minutes, then slice on the diagonal into medallions.

6 To make the vinaigrette, whisk together the lemon juice, honey and mustard, then add the vinegar and olive oil to taste. Season with salt and pepper.

7 Bring a saucepan of salted water to the boil, then reduce to a simmer. Blanch the baby carrots for 2 minutes, then add the asparagus and cook until tender. Drain. Toss with the pine nuts and season.

8 Place a quenelle of mash to one side of each serving plate and arrange the meat around it. Pile the vegetables on the side and spoon the vinaigrette over.

Bombay-style curried crab with jeera (cumin) rice

My inspiration for this dish comes from a visit to Singapore when I was about 10. I remember trying one of Singapore's most famous dishes, Singapore Chilli Crab, at an outdoor food market. I was hooked. Due to the relatively small size of our paddle crabs compared to the Singapore variants, I add tomatoes and onions to this dish when I cook it, similar to the way I would make a chicken curry. Over the years I have refined the dish to include spices such as cardamom and star anise. These two ingredients leave a sweet, pungent yet subtle and delicate taste on the palate. This is quite a messy and hands-on dish, and is great to share with friends. Tip: Garnish with heaps of coriander. Live to eat, don't eat to live!

Recipe by Arjay Magan
Serves 3–4
Preparation time: 15 minutes
Cooking time: 1 hour

8–10 medium paddle crabs
3 tsp vegetable oil
2 sticks cinnamon
5 star anise
6 cloves
6 green cardamom pods
15 curry leaves
3 bay leaves
2–3 medium onions, roughly
   chopped (more onions will result
   in a thicker curry)
1 tbsp finely chopped garlic
1 tbsp finely chopped ginger
1–2 tbsp finely chopped de-seeded
   green bird's-eye chillies
1 tbsp garam masala
4 tbsp fish masala (available from
   Asian stores)

1 Cut the crabs into quarters and clean. Crush the claws with the back of a knife for easy eating. Rinse and leave to drain.

2 In a high-sided saucepan heat the oil over a high heat until hot. Add the cinnamon, star anise, cloves and cardamom, and fry for 30 seconds. Add the curry leaves and bay leaves, and fry for 30 seconds.

3 Add the onions and fry on a low heat, stirring regularly, for 5–10 minutes or until soft and transparent. Do not brown the onion. Add the garlic, ginger and chilli, and cook for 1 minute. Add the garam masala and cook for a further minute.

4 Add the fish masala and cook for 5 minutes until the onion is a deep burnt-orange colour, allowing the flavours of the spices to combine in the pan and be absorbed by the onions. Season with salt.

5 After 5 minutes, add the chopped tomatoes and stir to combine. Cook for a further 5 minutes, then add the lemon juice and half the coriander. Bring to a simmer on a low heat. Place the crab in the pan, cover and gently cook for 20–30 minutes. The crab will actually cook in around 5 minutes, but the longer you leave it in the pan the more juices will run out, giving the curry a sweet crayfish-like flavour. The crab will not overcook as long as you cook it over a low heat.

(continued overleaf)

1 tsp salt
1–2 tins Wattie's Indian-style
  chopped tomatoes (1 for a dry
  curry or 2 for a soupy curry)
juice of ½ lemon
1 cup roughly chopped coriander
½ chopped red onion for serving

Rice
1 cup rice
1 tsp vegetable oil
1 bay leaf
2 cloves
6 curry leaves
1 tsp cumin seeds
½ tsp salt

6 To cook the rice, wash and rinse the rice thoroughly until the water runs clear, and drain. In a saucepan or rice cooker, heat the oil until hot. Add the bay leaf, cloves, curry leaves and cumin seeds and quickly fry for 20–30 seconds, stirring constantly. Add the rice and stir for 1 minute, then add 2 cups of water and the salt. Cook using the absorption method until the rice is done.

7 To serve, garnish the curry with the remaining coriander and the red onion. Place the rice in a side dish.

Rangiputa fragrant fish cakes with smoked capsicum and ginger salsa

This simple fish cake was my audition dish and I came up with it minutes before I entered the interview room to meet the judges for the first time. It's based on a special place I visited with lovely people, and to me this is the essence of memorable food: fabulous flavours in a wonderful setting eaten with interesting people. Rangiputa is a bach belonging to some friends, beside a west-facing harbour on the east coast in the Far North. One summer when we were visiting, we tasted tiny Thai fish cakes that someone had made. I've used a similar idea here to evoke the feeling of a laid-back summer party with friends beside the beach. The smoked capsicum and ginger salsa gives it a barbecue feel. I added crisp onion rings on top for texture. The recipe makes cakes that are quite fragile – add ½ cup of flour if you want them to be firmer. Chargrilled capsicums can be used in place of the smoked ones I've used here.

Recipe by Christine Hobbs
Serves 2 (or 6 fish cakes)
Preparation time: 1½ hours
Cooking time: 30 minutes

Fish cakes
400g fresh white fish
2 tbsp tom yum paste
½ cup coconut milk
½ cup chopped fresh coriander
  leaves
160g green beans, topped and finely
  sliced
juice of 1 lime
4 lemongrass stalks, bruised and
  finely chopped
½ cup plain flour
4 tbsp sesame seeds
4 tbsp vegetable oil
2 tsp sesame oil

Red capsicum salsa
1 cup manuka woodchips
½ cup jasmine tea
4 sprigs rosemary

1 To make the fish cakes, place the fish, tom yum paste and coconut milk in a food processor and pulse to a coarse consistency. Transfer to a bowl and combine with half the coriander, beans, lime juice and lemongrass. Mould the mixture into 6 large patties. Coat in flour, remaining coriander and sesame seeds. Set aside in the fridge for 1 hour.

2 To smoke the capsicum, line a wok with tinfoil and place the woodchips, jasmine tea and rosemary inside. Sit a cake rack on top. Place the capsicums on the rack, cover the wok with foil or a lid and place over a medium-high heat. Once the wok has heated up and the smoking is under way, lower the heat and leave for 30 minutes.

3 To make the salsa, remove the charred skin of the smoked capsicum and finely chop. Place in a bowl with the tomato, fresh capsicum, lime zest and juice, sweet chilli sauce and ginger, and combine. Season with salt and pepper.

4 To make the onion rings, place the sliced onion in a bowl and just cover with milk. Set aside for 15 minutes, then drain and dry thoroughly with paper towels. Place the onion rings in a small heavy-based frying pan and just cover with oil. Place over a high heat until the oil starts to boil, then reduce the heat to a simmer and cook for 20 minutes, turning the rings frequently with a fork. To finish, turn up the heat and brown, while continuing to turn, until the onion rings are crisp. Drain on paper towels.

(continued overleaf)

2 red capsicums, halved and cored
2 tomato, blanched, de-seeded,
   peeled and finely chopped
4 tbsp de-seeded and chopped red
   capsicum
grated zest and juice of 1 lime
2 tsp sweet chilli sauce
6 cubes glacé ginger, finely
   chopped
salt and freshly ground black
   pepper

Onion rings
2 onions, thinly sliced into rings
   (discard small rings)
¾ cup milk
rice bran oil for frying

5 To cook the fish cakes, heat a heavy-based frying pan over a medium heat, add the vegetable and sesame oils and fry the fish cakes for 2 minutes on each side. Place in a medium oven (180°C) for 5 minutes.

6 To serve, place each fish cake on a plate, top with a generous spoonful of salsa, and finish with onion rings.

Pan-seared blue cod with Pernod cream, lemon zest-infused mash, garlic fennel and roast cherry tomatoes

For the MasterChef auditions I wanted to create something that showcased my passion for local food, seasonal produce and complementary flavours. The view from my kitchen window was my inspiration — the backdrop of the Kaikoura Coast, the herb garden and the vegetable patch. I love the combination of aniseed flavours from the fennel, chervil and Pernod, balanced with the creaminess of the sauce and zesty mash. Keep an eye on the fish stock as it's reducing — it can disappear in a flash. And be careful when setting the Pernod alight — there are better ways to trim your eyebrows! The auditions were daunting and the fantastic response from the judges brought tears to my eyes.

Recipe by Fiona Read

Serves 4
Preparation time: 15 minutes
Cooking time: 45 minutes

Lemon zest-infused mash

4 large Agria potatoes, peeled and diced
250ml cream
grated zest of 1 lemon
1 clove garlic, bruised
salt and freshly ground white pepper

Garlic fennel and roast tomatoes

2 bulbs fennel, trimmed and quartered (reserve the fronds)
60g butter
1 clove garlic, crushed
whole nutmeg, grated
20g Parmesan, grated
12 cherry tomatoes
extra-virgin olive oil for drizzling

Pernod cream

300ml fish stock
20g butter

1 To make the mash, place the potatoes in a saucepan and just cover with water. Put over a high heat and bring to the boil, then lower the heat and simmer until tender. Drain and return to the saucepan, placing over a low heat to steam any remaining moisture from the potatoes. Using a potato ricer, mash the potatoes. Place the cream, lemon zest and garlic in a saucepan, and put over a medium heat. Simmer for 3–5 minutes, then remove the garlic. Add some of the cream mixture to the potatoes and, using a wooden spoon, whip the potatoes. Add more cream and whip to a firm but creamy consistency. Season with salt and white pepper. Set aside.

2 Preheat the oven to 200°C.

3 Bring a saucepan of salted water to the boil, then reduce to a simmer and simmer the fennel until just cooked. Drain well, then place the fennel in an ovenproof dish. Heat a small saucepan over a low heat, add the butter and garlic, and cook for 3–5 minutes, allowing the garlic to slowly infuse into the butter. Do not let the garlic colour. Pour the mixture over the fennel, then sprinkle with the nutmeg and Parmesan. Bake in the oven for 10–15 minutes, making sure the garlic doesn't burn.

4 Place the cherry tomatoes in an ovenproof dish, drizzle with olive oil and season with salt and pepper. Roast in the oven for 6–8 minutes until soft but still holding their shape.

5 To make the Pernod cream, heat a saucepan over a medium-high heat and pour in the fish stock. Bring to the boil, turn down the heat to a simmer and reduce by half. Add the butter and stir until melted, then

(continued overleaf)

100ml Pernod
125ml cream
1 sprig lemon thyme
1 tbsp finely chopped chives
1 tbsp finely chopped flat-leaf
  parsley

¼ cup plain flour
4 fillets blue cod
20g butter
2 tbsp grapeseed oil
sea salt

pour in the Pernod and, if you want to, set it alight to burn off the alcohol. Reduce the heat and add the cream and lemon thyme, simmering until the sauce thickens enough to coat the back of a spoon. Remove the thyme sprig. Just before serving, finely chop the reserved fennel fronds, and stir in with the chives and parsley.

6 Place the flour in a shallow dish and season generously with salt and pepper. Pat the fish dry and lightly coat in the flour, dusting off the excess. Heat a frying pan over a medium heat, add the butter and grapeseed oil and, when the butter has finished foaming and is almost brown, cook the fillets skin side down for 2–3 minutes or until golden. Turn and fry a further few minutes until cooked.

7 To serve, spoon the mash into the centre of each plate and top with a fish fillet. Gently pour the sauce over the fish and around the plate. Place the tomatoes and fennel to one side.

Roasted bluenose with braised Puy lentils and salsa verde

Recipe by Pip Cobcroft
Serves 2
Preparation time: 15 minutes
Cooking time: 1 hour

Lentils

2 carrots, finely diced
2 sticks celery, finely diced
2 shallots, finely diced
2 small bulbs fennel, outer leaves
    discarded and finely diced
6 x 1cm strips lemon peel
2 tbsp finely chopped thyme leaves
2 cloves garlic, sliced
2 bay leaf
900ml beef stock, plus extra if needed
2 cups Puy lentils
4 tbsp balsamic glaze
40g butter
salt and freshly ground black pepper

Salsa verde

2 bunches coriander leaves, roughly
    chopped
4 bunches flat-leaf parsley leaves,
    roughly chopped
2 small bunches mint leaves,
    roughly chopped
2 cloves garlic, chopped
2 tbsp salted capers, soaked and
    drained
8 anchovy fillets
2 tbsp Dijon mustard
juice of 2 lemons
zest of 1 lemon
extra-virgin olive oil for mixing

4 100g bluenose fillets, skin on
2 cloves garlic, sliced
4 tbsp clarified butter
chilli oil for serving
lemon wedges for serving

1 To cook the lentils, heat an oiled saucepan over a medium heat and gently sauté the carrots, celery, shallots and fennel until soft, without colouring. Add the lemon peel, thyme, garlic, bay leaf and stock, and bring to the boil. Reduce the heat, add the lentils and simmer for 40 minutes or until the lentils are tender. Add more stock if needed to prevent the lentils drying out; they should be a soupy consistency. Just before serving, stir through the balsamic glaze and butter, and season with salt and pepper.

2 Preheat the oven to 220°C.

3 To make the salsa verde, place the herbs, garlic, capers, anchovies, mustard and lemon juice and zest in a food processor and process until finely chopped. With the motor still running, slowly pour in extra-virgin olive oil in a stream to make a thick sauce. Season with salt and pepper.

4 Cut the fish fillets into 10cm pieces, score the skin side 4–5 times, just cutting through the skin, and season both sides with salt and pepper. Heat an ovenproof frying pan over a medium heat, and cook the garlic in the clarified butter for 1 minute. Add the fish, skin side down, and sear for 1 minute. Spoon some of the butter over the fish, then carefully turn over and cook for a further minute. Place the pan in the oven and bake the fish for 5 minutes.

5 To serve, spoon the lentils into shallow bowls and place the fish on top. Top with salsa verde, drizzle with a little chilli oil and serve with lemon wedges on the side.

This dish is not a typical 'family' dish but one that many of my friends have had the pleasure of trying. Before entering MasterChef, I put together a four-course lunch with the dishes I thought I would put before the judges. My assiduous panel of lovely lunching ladies professed this dish to be an absolute crowd pleaser! I usually buy a whole bluenose from Seamart and ask the fishmongers there to clean and fillet it for me. This ensures the freshest fish and fillets with skin on. The trick with the fish is to cook it skin side down in a hot pan, basting it with the melted butter, turn it over quickly and finish it in a hot oven for a couple of minutes. The braised Puy lentils are a favourite of mine and were described by Ross Burden as 'sexy', much to his surprise. The balsamic glaze at the end gives them another layer of flavour that enhances the whole dish.

Pan-seared scallops on fennel purée with honey balsamic drizzle

Recipe by Robert Trathen
Serves 4
Preparation time: 10 minutes
Cooking time: 20 minutes

Fennel purée
40g butter
400g fennel, sliced (reserve fronds
  for serving)
200g leeks (white part only), sliced
2 cups milk
⅔ cup cream
4 cloves garlic, peeled
2 star anise
salt and freshly ground black
  pepper

Honey balsamic drizzle
⅔ cup balsamic vinegar
2 tsp honey
20g butter

24 fresh scallops
20g butter
2 lemons for garnish

1 To make the purée, heat a frying pan over a medium heat and melt the butter. Add the fennel and leeks, and sauté until soft, then add the milk, cream, garlic and star anise, and simmer for 5–7 minutes. Strain the mixture through a sieve, reserving the liquid and discarding the star anise. Place the fennel, leeks, and garlic in a bowl and, using a stick blender, blend to a purée with some of the reserved liquid. Season with salt and pepper, and strain once more through a fine sieve. Set aside.

2 To make the drizzle, heat a small saucepan over a medium heat and simmer the vinegar until reduced by half. Stir in the honey and butter. Set aside.

3 Pat dry the scallops and season with salt. Heat an oiled frying pan over a high heat and add the butter. Place the scallops in the hot pan and cook for 90 seconds on each side, turning only once.

4 To serve, spoon a line of the purée down the centre of each plate and top with a row of scallops. Drizzle with the honey balsamic and scatter the reserved fennel fronds over. Garnish with half a lemon.

I love making purées and I designed this one especially for the MasterChef audition. Fennel is not a commonly used ingredient and it complements seafood so well. The leeks gave the dish a nice background flavour and the judges were blown away by the flavours. Ross even demonstrated the recipe on TV One's Good Morning! Growing up in Nelson, I was lucky enough to eat scallops every season, so I thought they'd be the perfect partner for the purée. The sweetness of the honey balsamic gives it a beautiful finish.

Crisp-skin snapper with crab mash, seared scallops, and broad bean and citrus salad

Ellerslie Race Day
Serves 4
Preparation time: 20 minutes
Cooking time: 30 minutes

4 150g snapper fillets, skin on

Crab mash
3 potatoes, peeled and diced
pinch of salt
½ cup cream
30g butter
1 cup crab meat
1 tbsp finely chopped chives
salt and freshly ground black pepper

Broad bean and citrus salad
1 cup broad beans
2 oranges, peeled and segmented
2 ruby grapefruit, peeled and
  segmented
2 lemons, peeled and segmented
juice of 1 lemon
2 tsp chervil, roughly chopped
8 scallops, scored

lemon oil for serving
sprigs of chervil for serving

1 Pat the fillets dry and set aside in the fridge.

2 To make the mash, place the potatoes in a saucepan, cover with water and add a large pinch of salt. Put over a medium heat, bring to the boil, then reduce to a simmer. Simmer until tender and drain. Return to the pan and mash. Combine the cream and butter in another saucepan over a medium heat and bring to the boil. Reduce the heat slightly and stir in the crab meat and chives. Season with salt and pepper. Add to the mashed potato and mix together thoroughly. Set aside.

3 To make the salad, place the broad beans in a bowl and soak in warm water. Remove the skins and discard. Combine the orange, grapefruit and lemon segments, broad beans and chopped chervil in a bowl. Drizzle with the lemon juice and season with salt and pepper. Set aside until ready to serve.

4 Heat an oiled frying pan over a low heat, score the snapper skin and season with salt. Place in the pan skin side down and cook until golden and crisp. Press down with a fish slice to evenly cook the fillet. Turn and cook for a further 1–2 minutes.

5 Heat an oiled frying pan over a medium heat and sear the scallops for 20–30 seconds on each side. Don't touch the scallops while cooking and turn only once.

6 To serve, spoon the mash onto each plate and top with a snapper fillet, skin side up. Place 2 scallops on top, serve the salad around the mash and garnish with a sprig of chervil. Drizzle lemon oil over and around the salad.

The keys to a nice crispy skin on your piece of snapper are as follows: nice dry skin, seasoned with a little salt, skin side down in a very hot pan with a little oil. Cook for about a minute and a half, then turn and cook for another 30–60 seconds. The skin should be crispy and the flesh should be just cooked, moist and succulent. **Nigel Anderson, Ellerslie Challenge**

Raw fish salad

This dish was inspired by two very important people in my life. It is a popular salad of marinated fish that is called kokoda in Fiji, poisson cru in Tahiti and oka or ota in Samoa and Tonga. Most countries in Asia have their own spin on raw fish salads as well. One important thing to remember is to squeeze out all the excess lemon juice after marinating the fish. This is so you get more of a fish flavour when biting into the pieces instead of a mouth full of lemon juice. **Kelly Young, Villa Maria Challenge**

Recipe by Kelly Young, Nigel Anderson and Tracey Gunn
Serves 4–6
Preparation time: 20 minutes
Cooking time: 1 hour to chill

1kg gurnard fillets, diced
juice of 5 lemons or limes
sea salt to taste
2 spring onions, finely sliced
3 red capsicums, cored and finely diced
6 vine-ripened tomatoes, finely diced
⅓ cup caperberries, drained, rinsed and cut in half
¼ cup finely chopped flat-leaf parsley
2 tins 400ml coconut cream
2 limes for serving

1 Place the fish in a bowl, cover with lemon or lime juice and sprinkle with salt. Place in fridge for 40–60 minutes to marinate. Drain and squeeze dry with a clean tea towel.

2 Combine the spring onions, capsicums, tomatoes, caperberries and parsley in a bowl. Add the fish and coconut cream and mix. Season with salt and pepper. Chill in the fridge for 20 minutes.

3 To serve, spoon the salad into bowls and garnish with lime wedges. You can also serve the salad on lettuce leaves.

Smoked fish Caesar salad with quail eggs

Recipe by Kelly Young, Nigel Anderson and Tracey Gunn
Serves 4
Preparation time: 30 minutes
Cooking time: 15 minutes

2 slices prosciutto di Parma
2 slices white bread, crusts removed
  and cut into cubes
olive oil for frying
6 quail eggs

Dressing
1 clove garlic, crushed
2 anchovy fillets
2 egg yolks
½ tsp Dijon mustard
1 tbsp Lea & Perrins Worcestershire
  Sauce
1 tbsp lemon juice
150ml light olive oil

1kg smoked fish, torn into chunks
4 baby cos lettuces
shaved Parmesan for serving

1 Heat a frying pan over a medium heat, put in the prosciutto slices and fry until crisp. Remove from the pan, then add the bread and drizzle with olive oil. Fry until golden all over, turning frequently, then season with salt. Finely slice the crisp prosciutto. Set the croûtons and prosciutto aside.

2 Bring a saucepan of water to the boil, then reduce to a simmer. Soft-boil the quail eggs for 2 minutes. Remove from the hot water and place in a bowl of iced water. Peel.

3 To make the dressing, process the garlic, anchovies and egg yolks in a food processor. Add the mustard, Worcestershire Sauce and lemon juice and, with the motor still running, slowly drizzle in the olive oil to form a creamy sauce. Season to taste.

4 Place the prosciutto, croûtons and smoked fish in a bowl, and carefully mix in the dressing.

5 To serve, arrange the cos leaves in a large bowl and spoon the salad into the centre. Arrange the quail eggs on top and scatter with shaved Parmesan.

This recipe is a twist on the original caesar salad. The success of this dish is due to quality ingredients and putting some love into it. The croûtons need to be well-seasoned and gently fried in olive oil. The dressing needs just the right amount of anchovies and the quail eggs need to be soft-boiled and very carefully peeled. Prosciutto and parmesan cheese speak for themselves! We chose a mildly smoked fish with large moist flakes which the judges approved of as it added a complementary flavour to the dish. During the tasting part of the challenge we were asked where we thought the caesar salad originated from and we all replied 'Italy'. Wrong! Apparently it was created by a guy called Caesar who was in Mexico when he came up with the recipe, which goes to show how much of a learning experience MasterChef was.
Tracey Gunn, Villa Maria Challenge

John Dory roulade with salmon mousse and spinach

I feel like this dish was the star of this challenge. Tracey's chicken mousse got great reviews on episode 3 so we thought we would go with a salmon mousse. When we turned up to Villa Maria and saw it was a barbecue challenge, we started to have second thoughts about doing such a complicated dish. However, with the lid on, the barbecue acts as an oven and we realised we needed to pull out something special to win what I think was the most important challenge of them all. We needed to prove to everyone that we deserved a second chance — and we did. **Kelly Young, Villa Maria Challenge**

Recipe by Kelly Young, Nigel Anderson and Tracey Gunn
Serves 4–6
Preparation time: 30 minutes + 30 minutes to chill in fridge
Cooking time: 1 hour

400g salmon fillet, skin off, pin boned and roughly chopped
2 egg whites
¼ cup cream
salt and freshly ground black pepper
20 large spinach leaves
2 small fillets John Dory

White wine sauce
30g butter
1 onion, finely diced
1 stick celery, peeled and finely diced
1 carrot, peeled and finely diced
1 bay leaf
1 cup white wine
2 cups fish stock
¼ cup cream
30g chilled butter, diced

1 jar salmon caviar

1 Place the salmon, egg whites and cream in a food processor, and process until smooth. Season with salt and pepper. Put the mousse in the fridge for 20 minutes to set.

2 Bring a saucepan of salted water to the boil, then reduce to a simmer. Blanch the spinach leaves for 20 seconds, then drain on paper towels. Cut the John Dory fillets in half lengthwise.

3 Lay out a sheet of tinfoil on a flat surface and place half the spinach leaves across the foil, slightly overlapping each other. Spread half the mousse over two-thirds of the leaves. Place 2 half fillets, one on top of the other, across the middle and carefully roll, using the foil, then pull firmly and twist the ends to form a tight cylindrical shape. Repeat with remaining spinach, mousse and fish. Place in the fridge for 30 minutes.

4 Preheat a closed barbecue or oven to 180°C. Bake the roulades for 10–15 minutes or until just cooked. Rest the fish for 5 minutes.

5 To make the white wine sauce, heat a saucepan over a medium heat and add the butter. Lightly sauté, without colouring, the onion, celery, carrot and bay leaf until soft. Pour in the white wine and fish stock and simmer for 25–35 minutes until reduced by half. Strain the stock into a clean saucepan and place back over a medium heat. Whisk in the cream, then gradually whisk in the butter to form a thick, creamy sauce. Season with salt.

6 Unwrap the roulades and slice. Place the slices in the centre of serving plates and spoon the sauce over. Scatter with salmon caviar.

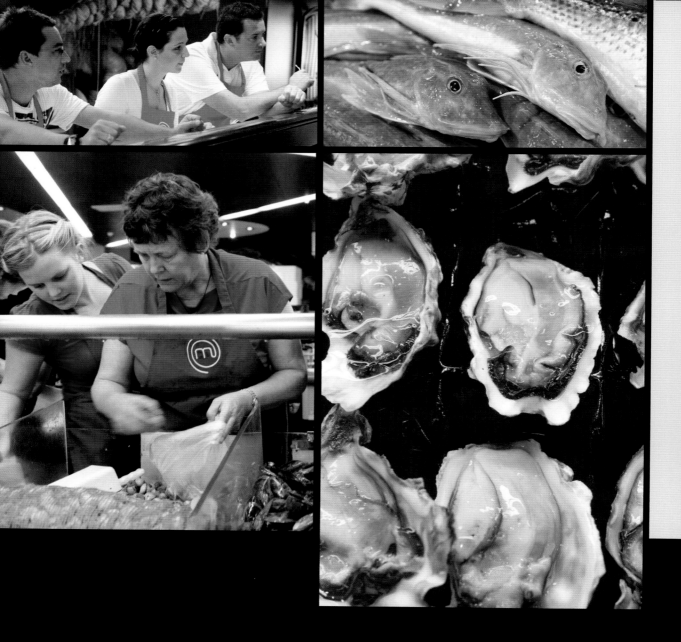

Crayfish with bisque sauce

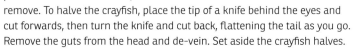

Recipe by Kelly Young, Nigel Anderson and Tracey Gunn
Serves 2
Preparation time: 15 minutes
Cooking time: 1 hour

1 medium crayfish
olive oil
2 fresh or frozen crayfish heads or
   shells, extra
1 onion, diced
1 large celery stick, diced
1 carrot, peeled and diced
1 bay leaf
2 sprigs thyme
1 400g tin tomatoes
2 tbsp tomato paste
1 litre fish stock
¼ cup cream
30ml brandy
salt and freshly ground black
   pepper

1 To cook the crayfish, bring a large saucepan of well-salted water to the boil. Add the whole crayfish to the pan and cook for 8 minutes, then remove. To halve the crayfish, place the tip of a knife behind the eyes and cut forwards, then turn the knife and cut back, flattening the tail as you go. Remove the guts from the head and de-vein. Set aside the crayfish halves.

2 To make the bisque, heat the oil in a large frying pan or heavy-based saucepan over a medium heat. Add the extra crayfish heads or shells to the pan and crush with a large mallet or potato masher. Fry over a medium heat until dark brown–orange, about 10 minutes.

3 Add the onion, celery and carrot to the pan and sauté for 10 minutes until soft. Then add the bay leaf, thyme, tomatoes and tomato paste and sauté for a further 5 minutes. Pour in the fish stock and simmer until the liquid is reduced by almost half, skimming off any scum as it forms. Strain the sauce through a fine sieve into a clean frying pan.

4 Stir in the cream and brandy, then reduce the sauce until it thickens, skimming any scum. Season with salt and pepper. Strain the sauce again.

5 Place the crayfish tails on a serving plate and arrange the heads on top. Pour the bisque over and serve.

Well, the crayfish was sensational — but the sauce wasn't quite what we were hoping for. Our intention was to cook the tails as the main substance of the dish and use the bodies for the major flavour element in our sauce. To cook the tails, we removed them from the bodies and inserted a wooden skewer down each side of the tail to stop it curling. These were then placed in salted water at a gentle simmer for 8 minutes.

The sauce was intended to be a rich bisque-style sauce. However, we presented an elegant, light, creamy crayfish sauce. Although not our intended result, it was a fantastic sauce and complemented the crayfish perfectly.

Note: This recipe uses extra crayfish heads for the bisque. If you do not have extra heads, you can cook the whole fresh crayfish, then remove the head to make the sauce and just serve the tails. **Nigel Anderson, Villa Maria Challenge**

Vanilla-scented scallop ravioli with a saffron lemon sauce

Recipe by Andrew Spear

Makes 6 ravioli

Preparation time: 30 minutes to chill pasta dough + 20 minutes

Cooking time: 45 minutes

pasta dough (see recipe on page 44)

16 fresh scallops, patted dry and finely diced
½ vanilla pod, split lengthwise and seeds scraped out
3 tbsp ricotta
salt and freshly ground black pepper
1 egg beaten

Saffron lemon sauce

4 shallots, finely diced
2 cloves garlic, finely diced
grated zest of ½ lemon
1 cup white wine
2 tbsp fresh thyme leaves
250ml cream
pinch of saffron, soaked in ½ cup water
30g butter
juice of 1 lemon

1 red capsicum, roasted and sliced, for serving
chopped flat-leaf parsley for serving

1 Prepare the pasta dough, following the recipe on page 44.

2 To make the filling, place the scallops, vanilla seeds and ricotta in a bowl and mix to combine. Season with salt and pepper.

3 To make the ravioli, cut the pasta dough in half and pass through a pasta machine, starting with the thickest setting and finishing with the finest, folding the pasta sheets in half each time. Repeat with the remaining half of the dough. Lay out the pasta sheets on a flat, floured surface and cut into 8cm rounds with a cookie cutter. Brush the edges of half the rounds with egg and place a heaped teaspoon of filling in the centre of each. Place another round on top and press the sides together to seal, removing all the air. Set aside.

4 To make the sauce, heat an oiled frying pan over a medium heat and sauté the shallots and garlic until soft. Add the lemon zest, wine and thyme, and simmer until the wine has almost evaporated. Add the cream and saffron and continue to reduce until the sauce is thick and coats the back of a spoon. Strain the sauce through a sieve into a jug and season with salt and pepper. Pour the sauce into a clean frying pan and place over a medium heat. Whisk the butter into the sauce until smooth and glossy and stir in the lemon juice.

5 Bring a saucepan of salted water to the boil and cook the ravioli in batches for 3–5 minutes or until they float to the surface. Remove with a slotted spoon.

6 To serve, place the ravioli on plates, spoon the sauce over and top with sliced capsicum and chopped parsley.

This dish is pretty much me on a plate. I love seafood and I love pasta, so I was always going to choose an audition dish that incorporated the two. The addition of vanilla and saffron adds a bit of an X factor, making the dish unique and special. Although it sounds strange, vanilla goes well with the sweet, dense meat of the scallops and a creamy saffron and lemon sauce is always going to be a winner. Go easy on the vanilla, though, because too much of it will seriously ruin the dish. It is great fun making ravioli, so take your time and enjoy it!

Venison loin with plum jus, tartiflette and broccolini

This is the meal I cooked at my audition which I hoped would impress the judges. I've always loved venison but until then had never attempted to cook it myself. A good piece of loin cooked medium–rare is a real treat and I devised a tart damson plum jus to complement its delicately rich flavour. The real star of the meal (according to the judges at least) was the tartiflette. A good friend of mine from France introduced me to it a while back. It's traditionally served as a main meal with crusty French bread, but for this meal I fancied it up a bit and served it in a kind of moulded stack alongside some fresh broccolini. Bon appétit.

Recipe by Mark Harvey
Serves 2
Preparation time: 8 hours to
    marinate venison + 15 minutes
Cooking time: 45 minutes

1 clove garlic, finely chopped
2 tbsp fresh thyme leaves
400g venison loin
olive oil for drizzling

Plum jus
½ onion, finely diced
1 tbsp butter
1 clove garlic, finely chopped
3 tbsp finely chopped smoked
    bacon lardons
½ cup red wine vinegar
3 tbsp red wine (Pinot Noir preferably)
1 cup beef stock
1 tbsp damson plum paste
1 Black Doris plum, stoned and sliced
3 sprigs thyme
salt and freshly ground black pepper

1 Combine the garlic and thyme in a bowl, add the venison loin and drizzle with olive oil. Coat the venison in the mixture and set aside in the fridge for at least 8 hours to marinate.

2 To make the plum jus, heat a frying pan over a low heat and gently sauté the onion in the butter until soft. Add the garlic and continue to sauté until the onion is soft but not caramelised. Place the bacon lardons in the frying pan and cook for 2–3 minutes. Pour in the vinegar and cook for 1 minute, then add the red wine and cook for a further minute. Add the beef stock, plum paste, plum and thyme, and simmer over a low heat for 10–15 minutes. Strain the plum jus through a sieve into a clean saucepan. Adjust the seasoning and keep on a low simmer.

3 Preheat the oven to 190°C.

4 To make the tartiflette, heat an oiled frying pan over a low heat and sauté the onion. Add the garlic and continue to sauté until the onion is soft but not caramelised. Place the potato in the pan and cook until golden. Pour in the white wine and season with salt and pepper. Cover and cook until the potato is tender, stirring occasionally.

5 Place a ring mould in the centre of a greased oven tray. Spoon the potato mixture into the mould until half full, top with a circle of reblochon, add more potato to fill the mould and top with another slice of reblochon, skin side up. Repeat for second one. Bake in the oven for 15–25 minutes or until the cheese is bubbling and foaming and slightly brown. Remove from the oven.

(continued overleaf)

Tartiflette

1 onion, finely diced

2 cloves garlic, finely chopped

2 potatoes, peeled and cubed

⅔ cup white wine (Viognier preferably)

1 80g round reblochon or brie cheese

pinch of sugar

8 pieces broccolini, sliced

8 hazelnuts, toasted and roughly chopped

1 tbsp roughly chopped flat-leaf parsley

6 Heat an oiled frying pan over a high heat. Sear the venison for 2–3 minutes on all sides, then place the pan in the oven for 5–6 minutes or until cooked to your liking. Remove and rest for 10 minutes. Cut into thick slices.

7 Bring a saucepan of lightly salted water to the boil and add a pinch of sugar. Reduce to a simmer and blanch the broccolini for 2–3 minutes. Refresh in a bowl of iced water.

8 Using a fish slice, carefully remove the tartiflettes from the tray and place in the centre of a plate. Use a sharp knife to cut around the mould edges and gently remove the mould. Arrange the venison around the potato. Place the broccolini to the side and top with the hazelnuts and parsley. Pour the jus over before serving.

Marinated venison with shallot cream and seasonal vegetables

I have always been a big fan of wild foods and seasonal fare. Much of this is sourced from my own garden, the Canterbury coastline, or the country areas within an hour or so from where I live. I learned while growing up that the secret when using any wild game or fish is to treat it with the respect and care it deserves. If you are preparing game, learn how long the meat should be aged for the best flavour and tenderness, and be bold enough to try a variety of sauces, vegetables and cooking methods to best complement the meat. The wild venison in my dish was harvested locally by a friend. The vegetables used were the pick of the season in terms of quality and availability, and the sauces were inspired by a masterful French cook I watched at work. These flavours are classic, but there is always room for your own personal touches in any dish.

Recipe by Stuart Walker

Serves 2
Preparation time: overnight to
   marinate venison + 20 minutes
Cooking time: 45 minutes

1 tbsp chopped rosemary leaves
1 tbsp chopped thyme leaves
4 juniper berries
1 clove garlic, crushed
400g venison loin
olive oil for drizzling

Shallot cream

40g butter
8 shallots, finely diced
1 cup chicken stock
1 cup cream
salt and freshly ground black
   pepper

Red wine sauce

1 cup red wine
½ cup beef stock
2 tsp Dijon mustard
100g butter, diced

1 Combine the rosemary, thyme, juniper berries and garlic in a bowl, add the venison and drizzle with olive oil. Coat the venison in the mixture well, place in a bag and tightly wrap in a cylindrical shape. Set aside in the fridge to marinate for 6–48 hours.

2 To make the shallot cream, heat a frying pan over a medium heat, add the butter and shallots and sauté until soft. Remove half the shallots and set aside. Pour the chicken stock into the pan, bring to a simmer and reduce by half. Stir in the cream and continue to reduce until the sauce coats the back of a spoon. Season with salt and pepper, and set aside.

3 To make the red wine sauce, heat a frying pan over a medium heat, add the reserved sautéed shallots and pour in the red wine. Simmer for 10 minutes, then add the beef stock and continue to reduce for a further 10 minutes. Add the mustard and whisk in the butter. Season with salt and pepper. Set aside.

4 To make the mushroom sauce, heat another frying pan over a medium heat and sauté the mushrooms in the butter until soft. Pour in the chicken stock and simmer until the sauce coats the back of a spoon. Set aside.

5 To make the mash, place the potatoes in a saucepan, cover with salted water and put over a high heat. Bring to the boil, then reduce to a simmer and cook until the potato is tender. Drain well. Add the butter, cream and garlic to the potato and mash until smooth. Season with salt and pepper. Set aside.

(continued overleaf)

Mushroom sauce

6 field mushrooms, sliced
20g butter
½ cup chicken stock

Mash

2 potatoes, peeled and diced
40g butter
½ cup cream
1 clove garlic, crushed

20g butter
2 field mushrooms
6 baby carrots
6 asparagus, trimmed

6 Preheat the oven to 190°C.

7 Heat an oiled ovenproof frying pan over a high heat. Season the venison with salt and pepper and sear for 2–3 minutes on each side, adding the mushrooms, then place in the oven for 5–6 minutes or until cooked to your liking. Rest for 5–10 minutes in a warm place then cut into medallions.

8 Add a knob of butter and the whole mushrooms to the pan the venison was cooked in and fry until soft. Season with salt and pepper.

9 Bring a saucepan of salted water to the boil, reduce to a simmer and blanch the baby carrots for 2 minutes, then add the asparagus for 1–2 minutes until tender. Drain, then drizzle with olive oil and season with salt and pepper.

10 To serve, spoon the mash onto plates and top with a field mushroom and venison slices. Drizzle with the red wine sauce. Pour the shallot cream to the side and arrange the asparagus, carrots and mushroom sauce over the top.

Potato nest on carrot, lemon and cumin purée with basil and cashew pesto and tomato salad

Recipe by Eva Gapski
Serves 2
Preparation time: 30 minutes
Cooking time: 35 minutes

10 cherry tomatoes, halved
1 spring onion, finely sliced
1 tbsp extra-virgin olive oil
1 tbsp balsamic vinegar

Carrot, lemon and cumin purée
3 large carrots, peeled and sliced
   into 5mm rounds
½ tin white beans, rinsed and
   drained
½ tsp ground cumin
1 clove garlic
½ tsp smoked paprika
juice of ½ lemon
¼ cup extra-virgin olive oil

Potato nests
2 large potatoes, peeled
½ tsp fine sea salt
1 tbsp extra-virgin olive oil

Basil and cashew pesto
¾ cup cashews, toasted
1 clove garlic, crushed
2 tsp lemon juice
1 cup basil leaves
½ cup extra-virgin olive oil

1 Place the tomatoes, spring onion, olive oil and vinegar in a bowl and mix to combine. Set aside to marinate.

2 To make the purée, bring a saucepan of salted water to the boil and reduce to a simmer. Add the carrots, cook until tender, then drain. Place the white beans, cumin, garlic, paprika and lemon juice in a food processor and process until smooth. Add the carrots and slowly drizzle in the olive oil while the motor is running to process to a smooth purée. Set aside.

3 To make the potato nests, place the potatoes in a spiraliser and spiralise into long fettuccine-style spirals (or grate, using a grater). Squeeze out all the excess moisture using a clean tea towel. Sprinkle with salt. Heat an oiled frying pan over a medium-high heat, add the potato spirals and fry for 20–25 minutes or until browned and crisp, turning occasionally to cook all over.

4 To make the pesto, place the cashews, garlic and lemon juice in a food processor and process until the mixture resembles fine breadcrumbs. Add the basil leaves and, with the motor running, drizzle in the olive oil until the mixture is creamy but still has a little texture. Season with salt and pepper.

5 To serve, spoon the purée into the centre of each plate and top with the potato nest. Finish with the pesto and place the tomato salad on the side.

This dish was a totally new creation of mine that I came up with the night before the audition. I had tried out a number of different combinations of ingredients and flavours but nothing worked until that moment. It was important for me to use my spiraliser, as I thought it would bring some novelty to the dish and create a talking point. The dish itself means a lot to me, not only because it opened the doors into MasterChef but also because it was the first vegan creation of mine that made my meat-loving boyfriend lick his plate (and he never licks the plate). His approval really boosted my confidence to put it in front of the judges. Using smoked paprika powder provides great depth to the purée, and roasting the cashew nuts for the pesto makes them taste even nuttier. I received great feedback from Simon and Ray, who both loved the flavours and the fact that I presented a delicious creation within the limitations of it being vegan.

Gorgonzola tortellini with sage burnt butter and julienned apple

This recipe contains two of my favourite foods: cheese and pasta. One of the cheeses I used in this recipe (acido cagliata) is only available from Ben Ohau Road Cheese and may be hard to source. You can substitute this cheese with a mild, soft goat's cheese, or with ricotta, but I suggest adding a bit of lemon zest to give it the required tang. I added the apple julienne to the dish to give it some tartness and to cut through the richness. Enjoy!

Recipe by Tracey Gunn

Make 12 tortellini
Preparation time: 30 minutes to chill pasta dough + 30 minutes
Cooking time: 15 minutes

pasta dough (see recipe on page 44)

Filling

100g Gorgonzola Dolce
300g acido cagliata cheese or soft goat's cheese
freshly ground black pepper

1 Granny Smith apple, peeled, cored and julienned
juice of ½ lemon

Sage butter

100g unsalted butter
12 whole sage leaves
6 sliced sage leaves

1 Prepare the pasta dough, following the recipe on page 44.

2 Combine the cheeses in a bowl and season with pepper. Refrigerate.

3 Cut the pasta dough into 7cm–8cm rounds with a cookie cutter. Place a teaspoon of the filling in the centre of a round, wet the top half of the dough with water and fold up to form a crescent. Press the edges together, removing all the air, then wet the 2 ends of the crescent and bring together at the front to form a tortellini shape. Repeat with the remaining pasta and filling.

4 Place the apple in a bowl, cover with cold water and add the lemon juice. Set aside.

5 To make the sage butter, heat a frying pan over a medium heat, melt the butter and add the whole sage leaves. Fry until crisp, then drain on paper towels. Add the sliced sage leaves and continue to cook until the butter is golden brown and nutty.

6 Bring a saucepan of salted water to the boil, then reduce to a simmer. Cook the tortellini in batches for 1–2 minutes or until they float to the surface. Remove with a slotted spoon, then place in the pan with the browned butter and coat gently.

7 To serve, spoon the tortellini onto plates and drizzle with more browned butter. Top with the julienned apple and crisp whole sage leaves.

Quattro formaggi pie

Recipe by Robert Trathen
Serves 2
Preparation time: 30 minutes
Cooking time: 20 minutes

shortcrust pastry (see recipe on
  page 44)
30g butter
2 leeks, finely sliced
1 medium onion, finely sliced
2 cloves garlic, finely chopped
1 tsp finely chopped thyme
200g rindless bacon, diced
50g blue cheese, crumbled
4 eggs
salt and freshly ground black
  pepper
30g Parmesan, grated
30g vintage cheddar, grated
30g cheddar, grated

1. Preheat the oven to 180°C.

2 Prepare the pastry following the recipe on page 44. Line a 35cm x 10cm fluted rectangular tin and blind bake according to recipe.

3 Melt the butter in a saucepan over a low heat and sweat the leeks and onion until very soft. Add the garlic and thyme, and continue to cook for 3 minutes. Remove from the pan and set aside.

4 Place a frying pan on a high heat and fry the bacon until crisp. Set aside.

5 Scatter the leeks and onion, bacon and blue cheese over the cooked pastry shell.

6 Whisk the eggs in a bowl, season with salt and pepper, and pour over the ingredients in the base. Sprinkle the remaining cheeses evenly over the top. Bake the pie for 30 minutes or until golden.

This pie was based on a classic bacon and egg pie. I come from a large family and bacon and egg pie was a fantastic lunch or picnic treat. Having watched Mum cook this pie many times, I modified it by adding four cheeses. Mum always made a relish, which is the best accompaniment to this rich cheesy pie.

Desserts

Raspberry and white chocolate tiramisu

Recipe by Abbey Looker
Makes 4
Preparation time: 30 minutes
Cooking time: 30 minutes + 30
  minutes to chill

250g white chocolate, chopped,
  plus extra to serve
¼ cup cream
175g caster sugar
500g frozen raspberries, defrosted
2 tbsp Glayva (Scotch whisky
  liqueur)
8 ladyfinger sponge cakes
2 egg yolks
250g mascarpone
juice of ½ lemon
1 punnet raspberries, hulled

1 To melt the chocolate, bring a saucepan of water to the boil, then reduce to a simmer. Place the chocolate in a bowl that will fit snugly on the saucepan and put the bowl over the simmering water. Carefully melt the chocolate, making sure water doesn't get into the bowl. Whisk the cream into the chocolate until the mixture is glossy. Set aside.

2 To make the sugar syrup, put 120g of the sugar in a saucepan with ⅓ cup of water and place over a high heat. Boil until the sugar has dissolved.

3 Place the raspberries in a blender with 1 tablespoon of the Glayva and the sugar syrup, and blend to form a chunky mixture. Reserve three-quarters of the mixture and pass the remainder through a fine sieve. Set aside.

4 Soak the ladyfingers in the larger portion of the raspberry mixture.

5 To make the sabayon (sauce), whisk the egg yolks, remaining sugar and Glayva in a metal bowl until thick and pale. Place the bowl over a saucepan of simmering water and whisk until a figure-8 stirring motion holds its shape in the mixture. Cool for a few minutes. Fold in the mascarpone and gradually whisk in the chocolate mixture. Whisk in the lemon juice to taste.

6 Pour an eighth of the mascarpone mixture into the bottom of 4 ramekins or glasses. Top with a layer of soaked ladyfingers. Alternate the layers, finishing with the strained raspberry mixture. Place the ramekins in the fridge to chill for 30 minutes.

7 To serve, top with fresh raspberries and extra grated white chocolate.

I created this recipe when I was living with two friends: one loved tiramisu and the other didn't like coffee — so I wanted to please both! I was also looking for a way to maintain the luxurious creaminess of the dessert in a way that was lighter on the palate. A touch of lemon cuts through the creamy mascarpone; and the raspberries and Glayva balance the sweetness of the white chocolate. This results in a light, quick and simple version of the traditional tiramisu — perfect for summer entertaining.

Mars bar chocolate soufflé with raspberry coulis and crème fraîche

When I made this dish for the audition, I think my soufflé impressed the judges. I had only made it once before I entered the competition but stuck to the recipe, and it worked! Ross Burden gave me a tip to help the soufflé rise — to dust the inside of the ramekin with sugar. The sugar crystals give the mixture something to climb up the sides of the ramekin.

Recipe by Daniel Bristow

Makes 4
Preparation time: 30 minutes
Cooking time: 30 minutes

Soufflé

1 53g Mars bar
100g chocolate (70% cocoa),
 chopped
1 tsp instant coffee
1 tbsp warm water
190ml whole milk
2 tbsp cornflour
3 egg yolks
butter for greasing
sugar for dusting
6 egg whites
pinch of salt
2 tbsp caster sugar
icing sugar for dusting
crème fraîche for serving

Raspberry coulis

150g raspberries
juice of 1 lemon
3 tbsp icing sugar

1 Preheat the oven to 190°C. Place the Mars bar in the freezer for 20–25 minutes.

2 To melt the chocolate, bring a saucepan of water to the boil, then reduce to a simmer. Place the chocolate in a bowl that fits snugly over the saucepan and put the bowl over the simmering water. Carefully melt the chocolate, making sure water doesn't get into the bowl.

3 Dissolve the coffee in the warm water.

4 Place half the milk in a saucepan. Add the cornflour and mix until smooth. Pour in the remaining milk and place over a medium heat, stirring continuously until the mixture thickens. Add the chocolate mixture, coffee and the egg yolks, and mix well.

5 Grease 4 ramekins with butter and dust with sugar.

6 Place the egg whites with a pinch of salt in a bowl. Using a hand beater, whisk until soft peaks form, then sprinkle in the sugar and continue to beat to stiff peaks. Fold ⅓ of the whites into the chocolate mixture and combine well, then carefully fold in the remaining whites.

7 Cut the Mars bars into small pieces.

8 Pour the mixture into the ramekins until they are ⅓ full. Place a piece of Mars bar on top, then cover with more mixture. Bake for 12–15 minutes.

9 To make the coulis, place the raspberries, lemon juice and icing sugar in a blender and blend. Adjust the lemon juice or sugar to taste. Strain the coulis through a sieve to remove the raspberry seeds.

10 Dust the soufflés with icing sugar. Serve the crème fraîche on the side and drizzle with the coulis.

Chocolate and raspberry mud pies with sugar shards and raspberry coulis

This pie helped me get second place in the pie challenge and was my best-looking dish on the show. When doing sugar chards try using a fork that has some of the raspberry coulis on it before dipping in the sugar, so you end up with beautiful pink streaks through the sugar.

Recipe by Karyn Fisk
Makes 4 small pies
Preparation time: 15 minutes
 (excluding pastry)
Cooking time: 25 minutes

sweet shortcrust pastry (see recipe
 on page 44)

Mud pies
2 eggs
30g sugar
250ml cream
1 vanilla pod
100g chocolate (70% cocoa),
 chopped
2 punnets raspberries
icing sugar for dusting

Sugar shards
150g sugar
30g glucose
30ml water

Raspberry coulis
½ punnet raspberries
100ml water
2 tbsp sugar

1 Prepare the sweet shortcrust pastry, following the recipe on page 44. Divide pastry into four even sized pieces and cover with clingfilm. Refrigerate for 30 minutes. Line 4 small tart tins and blind bake according to the recipe.

2 Preheat the oven to 160°C.

3 Lightly whisk the eggs and sugar in a bowl. Set aside.

4 Bring the cream and vanilla pod to the boil in a saucepan. Remove from the heat. Split and scrape vanilla pod with a knife, add to cream and strain. Discard the pod.

5 Place the chocolate in another bowl and pour the hot cream over. Stir until the chocolate is completely melted.

6 Gently whisk the chocolate and cream mixture into the egg mixture. Transfer to a saucepan and return to the heat until the mixture just starts to thicken. Stir if necessary. Remove from the heat and strain into a bowl.

7 Scatter the raspberries over the pastry cases and pour the chocolate mixture over. Bake for 10–12 minutes until the filling is only slightly wobbly in the centre. Allow to cool.

8 To make the sugar shards, bring the sugar, glucose and water to the boil. Keep boiling until the hard-ball stage is reached (around 121°C). Drizzle the sugar using a spoon or fork onto a non-stick baking mat into the desired shapes.

9 To make the raspberry coulis, place the raspberries, water and sugar in a saucepan and bring to the boil. Purée using a stick blender or food processor, then strain through a sieve.

10 To serve, place a pie on each plate, lightly dust with icing sugar and arrange the sugar shards on top. Drizzle with coulis.

Chocolate fudge cake with olive oil chocolate mousse and fresh raspberries

Ellerslie Race Day
Serves 12
Preparation time: 30 minutes
Cooking time: 1½ hours

Chocolate fudge cake
100g cocoa
200g butter, melted
400g caster sugar
4 eggs
1 tsp vanilla
90g plain flour
1 tsp baking powder
200g dark chocolate melts

Olive oil chocolate mousse
200g chocolate melts or roughly
  chopped chocolate
½ cup olive oil
200ml cream, whipped

fresh raspberries, hulled, for
  serving
icing sugar for dusting

1 Preheat the oven to 150°C. Grease a 20cm x 30cm cake tin and dust with flour.

2 To make the chocolate fudge cake, sift the cocoa into a medium-sized bowl. Add the butter, sugar, eggs and vanilla, and mix until smooth. Sift in the flour and baking powder, add the chocolate melts and fold into mixture to combine. Pour the mixture into the cake tin and bake for 45–50 minutes or until cooked. Cool in the tin, then cut into 12 slices.

3 To make the mousse, bring a saucepan of water to the boil, then reduce to a simmer. Place the chocolate melts in a bowl that fits snugly over the pan and put the bowl over the simmering water. Carefully melt the chocolate, making sure it doesn't burn. Slowly drizzle the olive oil into the chocolate, whisking continuously until the mixture is thick and glossy. Cool to room temperature, then fold in the whipped cream, one-third at a time. Refrigerate until ready to serve.

4 Serve slices of the cake topped with a quenelle of mousse. Scatter fresh berries on the side and dust with icing sugar.

This recipe warrants using good chocolate. It pays to spend a bit more on quality. You can also use a flavoured block of chocolate and cut into smaller pieces.

I think that the recipe should be slightly under-cooked for better consistency. This way, it is easier to cut with a fork, and served slightly warm it is delicious.

Judge Ray thought my cake was a little over-done, so be aware of the cooking time. **Sue Drummond, Ellerslie Challenge**

Vanilla crème brûlée with Champagne mint strawberries and macadamia and white chocolate cookies

Ellerslie Race Day

Makes 12 brûlées and 30 cookies
Preparation time: 1 hour to chill
  cookie dough + 30 minutes
Cooking time: 1½ hours

1 punnet strawberries, hulled and
  quartered
small bunch fresh mint leaves, torn
squeeze of orange juice
Champagne for soaking

Créme brûlée

12 egg yolks
185g caster sugar, plus extra for
  caramelising
1 litre cream
2 vanilla pods, split lengthwise and
  seeds scraped out

Macadamia and white chocolate
  cookies

125g butter
300g brown sugar
1 tsp vanilla extract
1 egg, lightly beaten
225g plain flour, sifted
200g macadamia nuts, lightly
  toasted and roughly chopped
250g white chocolate melts

1 Preheat the oven to 130°C.

2 Combine the strawberries and mint in a bowl. Squeeze orange juice over and cover with Champagne. Set aside.

3 To make the brûlées, whisk the egg yolks and sugar in a bowl until just combined.

4 Pour the cream into a saucepan and add the vanilla pods and seeds. Place over a medium-low heat and bring to the boil. Gently simmer for 3 minutes, then set aside to cool.

5 Discard the vanilla pods, then slowly pour one-quarter of the cooled cream into the egg mixture, whisking continuously and thoroughly. Continue whisking and add the rest of the cream mixture. Sieve into a clean bowl and allow to sit for a few minutes. Skim off any surface bubbles. Transfer to a jug and carefully pour into 12 ramekins.

6 Arrange the ramekins in a roasting tray and pour in boiling water so it comes three-quarters of the way up the sides of the ramekins. Cover the tray with tinfoil and pierce with 10 holes to allow the steam to escape. Bake for 30 minutes, checking regularly. The brûlées should be set but still have a slight wobble in the centre. Set aside to cool, then refrigerate.

7 To make the cookies, preheat the oven to 180°C. Line a baking tray with baking paper.

8 Using a hand beater, beat the butter, sugar and vanilla in a bowl until light and creamy. Add the egg, and continue to beat until well combined. Fold in the flour, then carefully stir in the nuts and chocolate until just combined. Roll into a cylindrical shape and wrap in clingfilm. Refrigerate for 45–60 minutes until firm.

9 Remove the clingfilm, cut the cookie dough into 1cm slices and place on the lined tray. Bake for 12–15 minutes or until golden. Leave on the tray for a few minutes before transferring to a wire rack to cool.

10 Just before serving, sprinkle the top of each brûlée with 1½ teaspoons of sugar. Smooth with the back of a spoon. With a blowtorch, or under a hot grill, carefully caramelise the sugar. Spoon the minted strawberries into a glass.

11 Arrange each brûlée on a plate with minted strawberries and cookies.

Chocolate, orange and pistachio marquise with poached rhubarb, raspberry marshmallow and chocolate and vanilla tuiles

Recipe by Mathew Metcalfe
Icing on The Cake Ltd
Serves 4
Preparation time: 2 ½–3 hours

Marquise

300g Valrhona dark chocolate (70% cocoa), broken into pieces
150g unsalted butter, softened
150g caster sugar
6 tbsp cocoa powder
6 eggs
300ml cream
grated zest of 1 orange
½ cup roasted pistachios, roughly chopped

Marshmallow

cornflour for dusting
½ cup water
21g gelatin powder
2 cups sugar
½ cup water
250g glucose
¼ tsp salt
2 tsp vanilla essence
4 tbsp raspberry powder

1 To make the marquise, bring a saucepan of water to the boil, then reduce to a simmer. Place the chocolate in a bowl that fits tightly over the saucepan and put over the simmering water. Be careful not to get any water in the chocolate. Gently heat until the chocolate has melted, then take off the heat and leave to cool a little.

2 Place the butter and half the sugar in a large bowl. Using an electric hand beater, beat until the mixture is really light and creamy. Then beat in the cocoa powder. Set aside.

3 Separate the eggs and put the yolks in a separate bowl, reserving the egg whites for the tuile. Pour in the remaining sugar and beat with an electric hand beater until pale and creamy and a figure-8 made with the beater holds its shape for a moment.

4 In another bowl, whip the cream until soft peaks form.

5 Pour the cooled chocolate into the butter mixture and carefully stir until well combined, then gently fold in the egg mixture. Stir in the orange zest and pistachios. When all the ingredients are amalgamated, stir in the whipped cream. Pour the mixture into 4 moulds and place in the freezer for at least 5 hours. Then take out and place in the fridge 2 hours prior to serving.

6 To make the marshmallow, line a baking tray with baking paper and dust heavily with cornflour.

7 Bring the water to the boil in a saucepan, then add the gelatin powder, whisking thoroughly until smooth and lump free.

8 Put the sugar, water, glucose, salt and vanilla in a saucepan placed over a high heat and bring to the boil. Boil for 40 seconds, then remove from the heat. Whisk in the gelatin mixture, then whisk in the raspberry powder. Pour the mixture into a cake mixer and beat on high for 13 minutes.

9 Spoon the marshmallow mixture into a piping bag and pipe small and

(continued overleaf)

Poached rhubarb

1 cup caster sugar
½ cup water
3 tbsp orange liqueur
juice of 1 orange, strained
2 thin sticks rhubarb, strings
   removed and cut into 3cm batons

Tuiles

100g plain flour
100g icing sugar
100g unsalted butter, at room
   temperature
100g egg whites, at room
   temperature
2 tbsp Valrhona cocoa

Spun sugar

½ cup water
1 cup caster sugar
⅛ tsp cream of tartar

fresh mint sprigs for serving

large teardrop shapes onto the lined tray. Place in the fridge for 30 minutes or until set. Remove and dust heavily with cornflour. Leave for an additional 10 minutes before dusting off the excess cornflour with a clean, dry pastry brush.

10 To poach the rhubarb, place the sugar, water, orange liqueur and juice in a saucepan over a medium-high heat. Bring to the boil and boil for 4 minutes.

11 Add the rhubarb to the sugar syrup and remove from the heat. Cover and let the rhubarb poach until the syrup is cold. The rhubarb should be slightly al dente. Remove the rhubarb from the syrup and place in a bowl. Reserve the syrup.

12 Pour the syrup into a saucepan placed over a medium-high heat and bring to a gentle boil. Reduce until the syrup thickens, then remove and place the saucepan in a bowl of cold water to stop the cooking process.

13 To make the tuiles, preheat the oven to 180°C. Line a baking tray with baking paper or use a silicone baking mat.

14 Sift together the flour and icing sugar, then place in a food processor with the butter, processing to a fine crumb consistency. Add the egg whites while the motor is still running. Mix well to make a smooth paste. Divide the mixture into 2 separate bowls and whisk the cocoa into one lot of dough.

15 Using a palette knife, scoop out a little of the vanilla dough and spread over the template on the baking tray. Spoon the chocolate batter into a piping bag and pipe dots down the centre of each biscuit. Place in the oven and bake for 3–4 minutes or until light golden. Remove immediately from the tray with a spatula and leave to cool or create a curved shape by draping over a rolling pin while still warm.

16 To make the spun sugar, pour the water into a saucepan and place over a medium heat. Mix together the sugar and cream of tartar in a bowl. Carefully pour the mixture in a thin stream into the centre of the saucepan to form a low mound. Without stirring the water, use your fingers to pat the sugar mound down until it is entirely moistened. Any sugar at the edges of the pan will be safely below the water line.

17 Place a lid on the saucepan and cook for a few minutes without stirring. Lift the lid — the sugar should have completely dissolved and the syrup should look clear. Continue to cook, without stirring, until the syrup begins to colour slightly. If the syrup seems to be colouring unevenly, swirl the pan gently rather than stirring.

18 To test the caramel, collect a bead of syrup with a skewer and drop it onto an upturned white saucer. When the drop looks pale and amber, turn the heat to low. Paying close attention, continue to cook the syrup and test drops until the caramel has darkened to a slightly reddish amber colour. Immediately remove the pan from the heat and let the caramel cool and thicken for 1–2 minutes.

19 Dip the tip of a spoon in the caramel and lift it 30cm above the pan, watching how the caramel flows from the tip back into the pan. At first, the caramel will form very fine threads as it flows off the spoon, then, as it cools, it will flow more slowly and form thicker golden threads — this is perfect spun sugar. Continue to dip and lift the spoon until this happens.

20 When the caramel is ready, coat the spoon in a thickish amount and wave it over baking paper in alternate directions to form the desired trellis pattern. Once the pattern is layered, cut out the shape you desire with a knife. Be gentle when removing the cooled sugar, as it is delicate.

21 Place each marquise in the centre of a serving plate and use a blowtorch to carefully heat the mould and gently remove it. Place poached rhubarb on each side of the marquise and top each stack with a small marshmallow drop. Top the marquise with 2 tuiles, then spoon on some poached rhubarb. Place a large marshmallow drop on top of the rhubarb. Place the caramel trellis to the side and decorate with a mint sprig. Spoon a small amount of the reserved rhubarb reduction around the base of the marquise.

Lime custard and meringue pie with orange vanilla jus

Lime is hands down my favourite milkshake flavour — there's just something special and delicious about the way the zingy lime mixes with the creamy milk. When faced with making a pie, I wanted to do something a bit different and decided to turn my favourite milkshake into a custard for the filling. You can adjust the intensity of the lime flavour by adding more or less zest, but don't be tempted to add lime juice or your custard will split. The orange vanilla jus is a great sauce that will keep in the fridge for a few days and goes just as well on French toast, pancakes or pretty much any dessert for that matter.

Recipe by Kirsty Cardy

Makes 1 pie
Preparation time: 30 minutes
  (excluding pastry)
Cooking time: 15 minutes

sweet shortcrust pastry (recipe on
  page 44)

Lime filling

220ml cream
6 egg yolks
240g sugar
grated zest and juice of 8 limes

Meringue

300g sugar
100ml boiling water
5 egg whites

Orange vanilla jus

juice of 3 oranges
½ vanilla pod, seeds scraped out

1 Prepare the pastry following the recipe for sweet shortcrust pastry on page 44. Roll out the pastry to fit a 10cm x 35cm rectangular fluted tin and blind bake according to recipe.

2 Preheat the oven to 150°C.

3 To make the filling, pour the cream into a saucepan and bring almost to the boil. Whisk the egg yolks, sugar and lime zest and juice in a bowl. Add up to 6 tablespoons, a tablespoon at a time, of the hot cream to the egg mix to 'temper' the filling, then whisk the remaining cream into the mixture.

4 Strain the filling into another bowl and pour into the baked pastry shell. Bake for 30–40 minutes or until set. Cool completely before topping with the meringue.

5 To make the meringue, bring the sugar and water to the boil in a saucepan over a high heat, then reduce the heat and simmer until it reaches the soft-ball stage (about 117°C).

6 Whisk the egg whites to stiff peaks. Slowly drizzle in the sugar syrup while still beating the egg whites. Continue beating until cool.

7 Spoon the meringue into a piping bag fitted with the largest nozzle. Pipe dollops onto the set custard. Brown lightly with a blowtorch or place under a hot grill.

8 To make the jus, place the orange juice and the vanilla seeds in a saucepan over a medium heat. Simmer until the liquid reduces and thickens. Strain to remove the pulp.

9 Cut slices of the pie and serve with the jus.

Almond, hazelnut and Brazil nut pie

Recipe by Brett McGregor
Makes 1 pie
Preparation time: 30 minutes
 (excluding pastry)
Cooking time: 25–30 minutes

sweet shortcrust pastry (see recipe
 on page 44); replace 25g of flour
 with 25g of cocoa
90g almonds, coarsely chopped
90g hazelnuts, coarsely chopped
90g Brazil nuts, coarsely chopped
3 eggs
60g brown sugar
4 tsp golden syrup
2 tsp vanilla essence
whipped cream for serving

1 Prepare the pastry, amending the
recipe by replacing 25g of the flour
with 25g of cocoa. Roll out the pastry to line a 22cm round pie dish and
blind bake according to recipe.

2 Preheat the oven to 180°C.

3 Scatter the nuts over the cooked pastry shell.

4 Lightly whisk the eggs in a bowl. Add the brown sugar, golden syrup and
vanilla, and mix well.

5 Pour the mixture over the nuts. Bake for 20–25 minutes or until the nuts
are golden brown.

6 Cut into wedges and serve with whipped cream.

*I have to admit this was a real test for me, as originally I thought of
making a pecan pie — I just couldn't locate the right ingredients in
the pantry. So I had to think on my feet — I decided to use other nuts
to replace the pecans. The chocolate pastry was delicious, too, and I
especially loved the gooey filling of this pie.*

Apple, rhubarb, prune and blueberry crumble pie

Recipe by Nigel Anderson

Makes 1 crumble pie
Preparation time: 20 minutes
  (excluding pastry)
Cooking time: 30 minutes

sweet shortcrust pastry (see recipe
  on page 44)
2 Granny Smith apples, peeled,
  cored and sliced
6 stalks rhubarb, strings removed
  and cut into 3cm pieces
6 pitted prunes, halved
¼ cup brown sugar

Crumble topping

⅓ cup brown sugar
⅓ cup flour
75g ground almonds
¾ cup rolled oats
50g butter, diced

1 cup fresh blueberries
cream or ice-cream for serving

1 Prepare the pastry following the recipe for sweet shortcrust pastry on page 44. Roll out to fit a 22cm round pie dish and blind bake according to the recipe.

2 Preheat the oven to 180°C.

3 Place the apples, rhubarb and prunes in a saucepan with a little water and the brown sugar, and gently simmer until just starting to soften.

4 To make the crumble topping, mix the brown sugar, flour, ground almonds and rolled oats together in a bowl. Rub the butter into the dried ingredients.

5 Pour the hot fruit and a little bit of liquid into the pastry shell. Sprinkle with the blueberries and top with the crumble mixture.

6 Bake for 20 minutes or until the topping is golden and crumbly.

7 Cut into wedges and serve with cream or ice-cream.

This dish was definitely inspired by Charlie, my wife. She is a fantastic crumble maker. Thanks to her I have learnt how to make a great crumble topping. Apple and rhubarb are classic partners, and the addition of prunes gives a unique extra dimension. The blueberries give some real freshness to the dish and when sprinkled over the fruit before adding the topping they burst through, giving spectacular presentation.

Antoine's raspberry roulade

Recipe by Tony Astle
Makes 1 roulade (8–10 portions)
Preparation time: 30 minutes
Cooking time: 30 minutes

6 egg whites
pinch of salt
1½ cups caster sugar
¾ tsp malt vinegar
1¾ tsp vanilla essence
2½ tbsp cornflour
2 tbsp icing sugar, plus extra for
  dusting
300ml cream
3 punnets fresh raspberries, hulled
  (reserve some for serving)
mint sprigs for garnishing

1 Preheat the oven to 180°C. Sprinkle a 23cm x 33cm Swiss roll tin with a little water and line with baking paper.

2 Place the egg whites in a bowl with a pinch of salt. Using an electric hand beater, beat to stiff peaks. Add the sugar gradually while continuing to beat. Then add the vinegar, ¾ tsp of vanilla and cornflour while continuing to beat the mixture. The peaks must be stiff.

3 Roughly spread the meringue over the lined tin. Bake in the oven for 12 minutes.

4 Cool in the tray, then invert onto a non-stick baking sheet that has been lightly dusted with icing sugar.

5 Whip the cream and the remaining vanilla in a bowl.

6 Spread three-quarters of the meringue with the cream. Top the cream with half the raspberries. Carefully roll up the roulade.

7 To make the coulis, place a punnet of raspberries in a small saucepan with a little water and sugar to taste. Simmer gently to break down the raspberries. Using a stick blender, blend the berries to make a coulis. Pass through a sieve and set aside to cool.

8 Place a thick slice of roulade in the centre of each plate. Spoon small amounts of the coulis around the roulade and arrange raspberries between the coulis. Dust the berries with icing sugar and garnish with a sprig of mint.

Pineapple pleaser

This is definitely one of my favourite dishes I did on MasterChef. Serve the rice in the basket at the last minute to prevent the basket from softening. It is an elegant yet easy dessert to prepare if you want to impress your guests.

Recipe by Kelly Young

Serves 4–6
Preparation time: 20 minutes
Cooking time: 1 hour

Pineapple wafer

80g unsalted butter
⅓ cup plain flour
1⅓ cups icing sugar
75g fresh pineapple, finely diced

Pineapple rice

600ml milk, plus extra if needed
½ cup caster sugar
½ vanilla pod
½ cinnamon stick
50g risotto rice (such as arborio)
1 egg yolk
¼ cup cream
75g fresh pineapple, finely diced

Grilled pineapple

olive oil for brushing
fresh pineapple, cut into 1cm-thick
   slices

Purée

½ cup brown sugar
½ cup water
30ml dark rum
1 star anise
4 mint leaves, plus extra sprigs for
   serving
½ mango, puréed

1 Preheat the oven to 170°C. Line a baking tray with baking paper and lightly grease the outside of 6 ramekins.

2 To make the wafers, process the butter, flour, icing sugar and pineapple in a food processor until smooth. Spread the mixture across the baking tray and cut out 6 x 8cm circles with a cookie cutter.

3 Bake for 8–10 minutes or until golden. Allow to cool for 30 seconds, then place over the upturned ramekins while warm and mould carefully to form baskets. Leave to set.

4 To make the pineapple rice, heat a saucepan over a medium heat and add the milk, sugar, vanilla pod, cinnamon stick and rice. Bring to the boil. Reduce the heat and simmer until the liquid has absorbed and the rice is creamy, stirring occasionally. Add more milk if required. Remove from the heat and discard the cinnamon stick and vanilla pod.

5 Mix the egg yolk and cream in a bowl and pour into the rice. Return the saucepan to a low heat and cook for a further minute, stirring continuously. Remove from heat and fold through the pineapple. Set aside.

6 To grill the pineapple, heat a griddle pan to a high heat and brush with olive oil. Cut the pineapple slices into quarters and cook each side for 1–2 minutes or until golden. Set aside.

7 To make the purée, combine the sugar, water, rum, star anise and mint leaves in a saucepan and place over a medium heat. Bring to the boil, then reduce to a simmer and simmer until the syrup thickens. Set aside to cool. Fold in the mango purée.

8 To serve, place a pineapple wafer to one side of each plate. Spoon the rice into the wafer and top with a mint sprig. Arrange the grilled pineapple slices on the side and, using a palette knife, elegantly smear the purée on the plate.

Mathew Metcalfe's chocolate cake

Recipe by Mathew Metcalfe
Icing on The Cake Ltd
Makes 1 sponge cake
Preparation time: 15 minutes
Cooking time: 2 hours

2 cups flour
2 cups sugar
¾ cup cocoa
2 tsp baking soda
2 large eggs
1 tsp salt
1 cup buttermilk
1 cup sunflower oil
1 tsp vanilla
1 cup boiling water

1 Preheat the oven to 145°C. Grease the base and sides of a 20cm springform tin and line the base with baking paper.

2 Place all the ingredients except the boiling water in the bowl of a cake mixer and combine on a low speed. Then add the boiling water and mix immediately on low speed until combined.

3 Pour the mixture into the prepared tin and bake in the oven for 1 hour 40 minutes or until a skewer inserted in the centre of the cake comes out clean.

4 Rest the cake in the tin for 30 minutes before removing to ensure the cake stays together.

5 Serve with a chocolate ganache if desired.

Croquembouche

Recipe by MasterChef kitchen
Serves 20–30 people
Preparation time: 3 hours
Cooking time: 1½ hours

Custard
1.3 litres milk
3 vanilla pods
320g egg yolks
1⅓ cups sugar
1 cup cornflour
125g unsalted butter, chopped

Choux pastry
400g unsalted butter, chopped
955ml water
1 tbsp sugar
1 tbsp salt
3½ cups plain flour, sifted
16 eggs

Caramel
400ml water
6 cups sugar
500 ml glucose

white sugar crystals for dipping
fresh raspberries for serving

1 To make the custard, split the vanilla pods in half lengthwise and place them with the milk in a saucepan over a low heat. Bring it gently to the boil, then remove from the heat. Take out the vanilla pods.

2 Beat the egg yolks, sugar and cornflour in a bowl until thick, and gradually whisk in the milk. Heat the mixture over a medium heat. Stir until the custard gets thick. Put it in a bowl, add the butter and then leave the custard to cool. Put it in the fridge while you make the choux pastry.

3 Preheat the oven to 210°C.

4 To make the choux pastry, first grease the oven trays. Place the butter, water, sugar and salt into a large saucepan and bring the mixture to the boil. Remove from the heat and quickly beat in the flour. Continue beating the mixture over a low heat until it pulls away from the sides of the pan. Cook for a further minute over a low heat.

5 Beat the pastry with a mixer. Gradually add the eggs, one at a time. Beat well until the mixture is smooth and thick.

6 Using a piping bag, put rounds of the mixture onto oven trays, spacing them well apart. Bake for approximately 30 minutes, or until they are hollow-sounding when you tap them. Leave them to cool.

7 Use a piping bag to fill each puff, through its base, with custard.

8 To make the caramel, combine water and sugar in a saucepan and bring to the boil. Add the glucose and cook until the mixture is amber in colour. Remove from the heat and place on a cool surface to stop it cooking.

9 To make a base for your croquembouche, grease a large frying pan and pour in enough caramel to cover the base of the pan. Leave it to cool.

10 Line a baking tray with baking paper. When you're ready to assemble the croquembouche, dip the bases of about one-quarter of the puffs in the caramel, coating them well. Pour the sugar crystals into a bowl and dip the puffs in to coat them. Allow to set.

(continued overleaf)

11 To assemble, lightly brush the inside of the croquembouche cone with oil. Dip the sides of the rest of the puffs in the caramel one at a time and place inside the cone. Begin by dividing the cone into quarters and placing the puffs in lines starting from the top and working down to the base. Continue adding the balls until the cone is covered. Use the puffs coated with sugar crystals to create a spiral pattern around the cone.

12 Take the base of the croquembouche out of the pan. Spread a little caramel on the base. Carefully put the cone upside down onto the caramel base and lightly tap with a wooden spoon to gently remove the croquembouche.

13 Gently heat the remaining caramel. Meanwhile, decorate the croquembouche with fresh raspberries. Lay out baking paper on a flat surface. Dip 2 forks into the caramel and spin across the baking paper to form a thin veil. Carefully pick up the veil and wrap around the croquembouche.

similar to sour cream, but richer and higher in fat. It has a culture added to it that gives it a characteristic tangy flavour.

demitasse cup A French term for half cup. Either a tiny coffee cup or the very strong black coffee served in the cup.

furikake This is a dry Japanese condiment used to flavour rice. It typically consists of a mixture of dried and ground fish, sesame seeds, chopped seaweed, sugar, salt and monosodium glutamate. Available from most Asian food shops.

Glayva This Scottish liqueur is made with Scotch whisky, honey and a well-guarded herbal formula.

Gorgonzola dolce This is a milder version of aged Gorgonzola.

lardons, bacon A French term which refers to bacon that has been sliced and fried.

lemon oil An essential oil extracted from lemon peel and mixed with olive oil, which can be used in food flavouring.

manuka dust Sawdust from manuka wood, used for smoking.

micro-greens Young shoots of salad greens, which usually have just the first two leaves. Used to garnish.

orange oil An essential oil extracted from orange peel and mixed with olive oil, which can be used in food flavouring.

Pacojet This appliance mixes and purées deep frozen food directly in its frozen state, without thawing it. This produces a frozen and natural tasting mousse of fine consistency to ideal serving temperature.

palette knife The flexibility of a palette knife (also known as a frosting spatula) allows it to easily slide underneath pastries or similar items.

pomegranate molasses Pomegranate molasses, or syrup, is made from cooked-down, or reduced pomegranate juice.

quenelle A light, delicate dumpling or mixture formed into small ovals.

raspberry powder A powder made from freeze-dried raspberries which retains the natural colour and intense flavour of the fresh fruit.

sabayon The French term for zabaglione — a dessert made by whisking together egg yolks, wine (traditionally Marsala) and sugar.

Acknowledgements

savoury chocolate Dark chocolate infused with savoury spices. Usually 72% cocoa.

Shaoxing wine A Chinese wine fermented from rice that is drunk as a beverage and used in cooking, especially for marinating meats. Available from Asian food shops.

spiraliser This gadget allows you to create spaghetti and spiral shapes from vegetables and fruit.

Thank you very much to the following people for the contributions they all made to this book:

To the *MasterChef New Zealand* top twelve contestants for contributing their recipes and notes: Nigel Anderson, Kirsty Cardy, Sue Drummond, Karyn Fisk, Tracey Gunn, Mark Harvey, Christine Hobbs, Brett McGregor, Steve Juergens, Andrew Spear, Rob Trathen and Kelly Young.

To the contestants who made it to the top twenty-four for their recipes and notes: Daniel Bristow, Pip Cobcroft, Eva Gapski, Carlos Garcia, Sarah Irvine, Abbey Looker, Fiona McDonald, Arjay Magan, Philip Maultsaid, Fiona Read, Stuart Walker and Kylie Wheeler.

To the chefs who contributed their recipes: Tony Astle of Antoines, Adrian Brett-Chinnery of Bracu, Simon Gault, Volker Marecek of The Langham, Mathew Metcalfe of Icing on the Cake Ltd and the MasterChef kitchen.

To the judges and guest chefs who appear in photographs: Ross Burden, Simon Gault, Ray McVinnie, Al Brown, Tony Astle, Josh Emmett, Michael Meredith, Judith Tabron and Simon Wright.

To Marc Zajtman especially, but also to Alyx Fausett and Ginny Grant for all their wonderful help testing and cooking the recipes for the marathon photoshoots. And to Tamara West for props and styling, and to The Studio of Tableware and Nest for providing products. Thanks also to Countdown for providing food for the photoshoots.

To Aaron McLean for the beautiful food photography.

To Frances Oliver for the amazing action photography and all shots of the contestants.

To designer Anna Seabrook for her elegant design and to Jenny Hellen and Nicola van Aardt at Random House New Zealand for bringing it all together.

To Ben Liebmann at FremantleMedia Australia and Darryl McEwen, Bettina Hollings and Cindi Lucas at Imagination TV for help and support throughout.

Index